#Unfiltered

Praise For

#Unfiltered

"In #UNFILTERED, Alissa pours out her heart from a truthful place that very few people have the courage to show. At times, she is broken and bitter; at other times, happy and hopeful. And it is ALL beautiful. She shares her journey—the experience of loss and devastation—and equips you to navigate disappointment and frustration in your own life. It is a must read!"
—**LISA BRUNSON**, international recording artist and worship leader

"The book you're holding in your hands is a living testimony of a woman who fought hell to experience heaven. As you read the pages of this book, you will be inspired, encouraged, strengthened, and filled with faith. The power of the message in this book is not simply Alissa's testimony but her ability to encourage you to believe that you're next!"
—**TONY SUAREZ**, international evangelist, Tony Suarez Ministries

"There has never been a truer title for what is within the pages of a book than in #UNFILTERED. It is real. It is raw. And it is relevant to anyone who has ever experienced things in life that they didn't expect to. Alissa writes honestly from the pages of her life; she captures the emotion of what it is to live through difficult times and how she conquered what was meant to conquer her."
—**GERMAINE BRUNSON**, international evangelist

"Take a journey of freedom, healing, and overcoming with Alissa Holt. Her raw and #UNFILTERED style will challenge you to stop accepting the masks of religion and walk into the fullness of God's freedom for your life!"

—**JOEL STOCKSTILL**, Executive director of Surge Project

#Unfiltered

WALKING THROUGH DIRT WHILE EMBRACING YOUR DESTINY

ALISSA HOLT

Published in the United States by Alissa Holt.

Cover design by Andrew Pealock (www.ampstudios.video)

First paperback edition April 2019

ISBN 978-1-7346320-0-2 (Trade Paperback)
ISBN 978-1-7346320-1-9 (eBook)

Printed in the United States of America
10 9 8 7 6 5 4 3 2 1

To my daughters, Kinsleigh and Aurora.
May you dance in your dirt—without apology—so that you can
embrace the destiny God has created you for.

Contents

Part 2

Foreword

Unfiltered. What an exquisite book. Listen … I wasn't ready. Even though that name alone speaks for itself, I was so moved, from beginning to end. This book is a must read. It will help you open up your heart to reveal any hidden places in your soul that need a touch from the Lord.

I found the truth behind it all is that it takes class participation to walk in complete healing. The enemy always wants us to drown in the heartbreak and stay there way longer than we should—feeling like we've been placed on the clearance rack, when God created us to be on the couture rack. This book #*UNFILTERED* will not let you stay down but will help you get up. The revelation in this book will set you free.

I've discovered that when we are at rock bottom, we find the Rock at the bottom, which is Jesus. He helps us get honest and see it for what it is. He helps us own it, deal with it, and heal it. The pain may not be our fault, but the healing is our responsibility. How easy it is to become a victim in our story, allowing a season in our life to define our whole lifetime. But truth is, life isn't always what we desired it would be. Sometimes our expectations are crushed, and we must dig deep to start over. Our desire to get better must be stronger than our desire to get bitter.

I love Alissa and her transparency. I have also walked through a divorce while having two children that needed their mama to get well, so I related so much to this book. I love every chapter and am honored to write this foreword. I believe in Alissa and every word written from her heart. She has done such a brilliant job with her raw real-talk on the steps you have to take to reclaim your self-esteem, your dignity, and your heart. Thank you, Alissa, for your yes. So very proud of you and all the people who are going to be set free and healed through your obedience with this book.

Much love,

Real Talk Kim

best-selling author and speaker

Introduction

What it do all my crew!

Here it is! The opening letter of my book. The part where I encourage you to read my pages. The part where I craft my heart, thoughts, intents, and desires in such a way that—I hope—it moves you to hashtag this book as your next #CurrentRead on your Instagram stories. What I write next will be a defining moment that determines whether this book is for you. It will leave you to decide whether you read on or reach for another book.

If I'm being honest, I feel as though I'm getting on a roller coaster ride, butt naked, and asking you to join me. We're standing in line waiting for the thrill of our life. But first, ladies and gentlemen, keep your hands and feet inside the ride, remain seated at all times, and please—for the love of coffee—remove your glasses because this will unfilter every lie that ever tried to keep you from living your best life.

Are you ready? Here we go ...

This book is a collection of confessions I never felt able to share within the church. It's filled with my personal journal entries that were written during the darkest seasons of my life, and it contains the one truth that will continually change everything you believe about where you're going and how to get there.

What is that truth exactly?

It's as close as your reflection in the mirror.

Friend, the truth is that you—and only you—are the answer to the healing, restoration, and promise for your life.

The stories filling these pages are from the pain behind rape, divorce, self-hate, illness, mental struggles, infertility, loss, and more. They're told from the far-too-convincing lies that God is a punisher of sins and promise can't be ours until all the pieces are put back in place. These stories unlock the truth behind what it looks like to walk through dirt while embracing destiny, and they unfilter the process behind the steps you must take to possess your promise.

I get messages from people all over the world, and the most asked question that I receive when tragedy hits someone's life is, "How do I move on when I don't understand why this happened?" Please hear me on this. You may not understand, but you'll never be able to move forward unless you embrace the life that's yours and stop denying the dirt. Denial doesn't build destiny … owning your dirt does.

Denial doesn't build destiny …

Owning your dirt does.

Let me ask this, How can you possess the promise when you refuse to address the lies that are stealing your identity?

You can never own your future until you start owning your now. Our number one problem as humans rests in our ability to accept the lies that tell us we are less than what we've been created to be. We see our life through a lens that is filtered with pain, rejection, abandonment, failure, flaws, and doctrine, and it leaves us with a distorted view of who we are.

When I found myself walking through divorce after nearly ten years of marriage, two baby girls, and a life of full-time ministry, I scrambled to cover up any sign of dirt that threatened to mark me as "dirty." With a pile of broken memories and a future filtered with pain, I reached an opportunity to learn just what it meant to be positioned toward promise as I allowed God to rebuild the pieces of my life.

As I'm writing you this letter, I'm sitting at my kitchen table, elbow deep in journals, reading over the pages of my life. The screensaver on my iPhone shows a picture of my husband and me celebrating one year of marriage this past April, and the sticky note on my computer says I only have twelve days left before I embrace the new decade of "thirty, flirty, and thriving."

I have coffee by my side, Demi Lovato's "Sorry Not Sorry" blaring in my ears, and I don't think there's a more perfect scenario than this moment for me to share my heart with you. This song formed the mantra of my life over the past two years, paired with Elevation Worship's "Do It Again." Although this playlist may not be what some consider typical, and probably won't get a solid stamp of approval by many, the fact remains that it's the one that got me through hell by reaffirming two truths to my heart, time and time again.

1. His promise still stands, no matter what I'm facing, and I can remain confident that his faithfulness is greater than my faults.

2. I am the baddest savage you will ever meet, and I'm sorry (but not
   sorry) that the fire inspired me to turn the table by taking my life
   back.

I'm at a much different place in my life right now. Love has found its
way back into my life, restoration has been found, ministry is growing,
and healing has taken place in my heart, all because I remembered who I
was (dirt and all) and changed the game. The process has not been easy,
but the evidence is enough for me to confidently say that owning my *now*
prepared me for my *tomorrow*.

I'm done apologizing for the dirt in my life, y'all, and I'm done
believing that *promise* is not mine! I made a vow to myself—long before
the promise of restoration or healing ever took place in my life—to not
allow any bit of my pain to go to waste. I promised myself that I would
make it my life's goal to show every person possible what it means to
embrace a life unfiltered and to walk in the freedom of who you truly are.
I told myself that every shattered piece would bring me purpose and
every bit of loss would launch me into my place called "There."

So if you're looking for truth, then here it is: Your promise is not
waiting for the best future version of yourself to arrive. Your destiny is
available for you right now and right here! The truth is, you decide
whether your dirt will disable you or empower you to own your life once
more! The truth is, you can blame others for the filth that marked you,
but that will leave you shackled to the broken pieces. The truth is,
brokenness can become the crutch that disables you from living a life of
freedom, or it can become the thing that deploys you into your destiny.

The truth is, the thing you experienced is not the source behind what's holding you back.

You had destiny written in your dirt long before you ever had a chance to be labeled as clean! You hold the shovel of purpose in your hands, friend, and you are the answer to your life! Are you willing to dig through the dirt by walking out your journey and embracing what God has for you?

I saw a quote on Pinterest right after my divorce finalized. It said this, "What if everything you're going through is preparing you for everything you have ever prayed for?" I don't know where you're at in life, but I do know you'll never move forward unless you're willing to unfilter the lies behind the dirt you're holding on to. Stop giving other people credit for destroying your future and start sorting through the wreckage with the Father. You can make a bed out of the shattered pieces of your life by choosing to live in brokenness, but that's not God's plan for you. You have to take responsibility for your future. You have to allow those pieces to become your tools for rebuilding and the foundation to build from.

This book is covered in dirt and shows the mark of destiny written within its pages. From personal loss, pain, and tragedy, I want to invite you to read of how the process of restoration and healing took place in my life while I walked down a dirty road and embraced my destiny.

Here's the deal. I don't know where you're at or how you got there, but I do know that you can choose where you're going. I don't know whose fault it was or how it happened, but I do know that you can live beyond the memory of yesterday by owning your tomorrow. I don't know who lied to you about what you're capable of, but I do know that you hold the power to shape the truth of who you are. I don't know what's been holding you back, but I do know that you're the answer to moving forward.

You are not dirty—you are destined. The question is, how long will you sit in the wreckage before you decide that it's time to build with the pieces?

It's not enough for someone else to believe in you. It's time for you to start believing in yourself. You're the answer to every promise, every dream, every call, and the destiny on your life. Stop waiting for some greater power to fix your pieces and start recognizing that Jesus can't touch what you don't allow him to!

Don't forget to share your #CurrentRead, small victories, and the journey of walking down whatever dirt-filled road you're on by joining the #UnfilteredDirt movement on social media. Whether it's a picture of you smiling for the first time in months or a snapshot of what it looks like for you to silence the lies and conquer your fears, let us celebrate with you by building a community that embraces our dirt and revels in our ability to walk #UNFILTERED and unapologetic!

So let's do this!

Go join that hashtag and let's show each other all the ways that we're walking in our destiny—DIRT AND ALL!

You are not dirty—you are destined.

Are you ready for more? Let me reach through these pages and take you by the hand as we walk down this road together to embrace a life of destiny unfiltered.

With all my love for coffee,

Alissa

Part 1

Walking Through Dirt

Journal entry

June 15, 2017

Hello,

New journals often signify something exciting and full of wonder as I wait to fill the pages with life, family, love, and God. But I'm not sure how to start off this new journey of my life. Everything looks so different now. And I've avoided journaling for the last month and a half due to the fear of what's staring me straight in the face.

People say to look for the silver lining in life, but as crazy as it may seem, I'm here to say I believe God is going to do much more than that for me. And I'll even go as far as to say he's fixing to reveal the gold.

My sister, Bethany, got me this journal that I'm writing in. I thought to myself, *How could this be any more perfect?* Inscribed on the front cover is the verse, "Trust in the Lord with all your heart," and the pages are beautifully lined with gold. It's reassuring to know God sees us right where we're at in life, and he sends us little reminders like these along the way.

Losing my husband was never something I thought I'd write about. Yet here I am, writing. I'm not sure where to start, but this journal makes it a little easier to remind myself that I'm trusting in God, because let's be real ... every ounce of me doesn't understand this one bit. What do you do when you wake up one day to a changed man? What do you do when life as you know it ends? What do you do when your reality is nothing like your intended hopes, desires, plans, and wishes? What do you do when the person you love the most decides that they don't love you back, and you can't change their mind?

I'm at a loss. I'm sick to my stomach. My heart feels like it has been chewed up, spit out, ran over a thousand times, and left for dead. I've never felt emotional pain on this level. I lay in bed at night feeling like my insides are dying, and all I can do is scream out in pain. My face stays buried in my pillow at night in hopes that I don't wake up the kids with my crying. It seems like that's all my pillow is good for lately, since I never sleep.

Anxiety pills. I always said I would never become "that person." But the silence of the night is nothing more than a screaming reminder that I have no idea where my husband is, where he's staying, who he's with, and that the kids and I are at home alone. So please ... give me another pill. I need to sleep, and Jesus will just have to understand.

My life has been stolen from me, and to be honest, I'm mad as hell! Who is this woman I've become and where is my life? It's torture loving someone who doesn't love you back. Someone who abandoned their vows and walked away. Someone who refuses to give you any answers and leaves you in the deafening silence to wonder what's going on in their mind.

Where do I go from here? What do I do next? How do I tell my kids? I don't know the answer, but I did meet with a divorce attorney today.

And sadly enough, today is also Kinsleigh's seventh birthday. I never, in a million years, thought I'd spend my beautiful baby girl's birthday trying to decide how to move forward without her daddy. Regardless, I needed some perspective. So I decided to at least sit down and talk, even if no decision was made yet.

Somehow, I'm still holding on to restoration. God can fix this, can't he? I'm not sure. But the truth is, at this moment I feel as though I'm in a literal fire. I can feel rage burning on the inside of me in ways I never thought was humanly possible. Abandonment, by the one person who was supposed to love, protect, and provide for me and our family, is one of the biggest forms of betrayal I've ever experienced ... and now I'm angry!

Still, even through my anger, somehow God speaks ... and I'm learning that transition causes a shift in perspective. If I refuse that shift, then I'll reject the new thing God's trying to bring me into.

So here I am, trying to tame the anger. Here I am, trying to scream a little less into my pillow at night. Here I am, trying to let my tears dry up a little more. Here I am, trying to put down the pills and embrace the shift of perspective and the new thing ahead of me ... whatever that is.

I don't understand it. It makes no sense to me. Surely God is not a God of divorce? Surely a broken family is not his plan for our life? Surely this is all wrong?

Still, I will continue to look for the gold in this dirt.

·

Funny enough, my Catholic lawyer said it the best. She pierced my heart, with her cigarette hanging out of her mouth, when her raspy voice spoke these words, "Is there such a thing as a Christian divorce? Is there such a thing as God allowing this to happen to you? I mean really, think about it. Maybe God is bigger than our religion can understand. Is it crazy to think that this was his plan all along, so you could finally be the badass woman you were always meant to be? What if your soon-to-be ex-husband was a part of the story, but wasn't a part of the bigger plan? I think this just might be God … but who am I? I'm just a crazy Catholic lawyer who likes to smoke."

I left that office with a shift in my mindset. Yes, I'm mad as hell, but I refuse to allow hell to drive me mad! I'm changing the game and embracing the change. I'm moving forward with uncertainty because it's not about what I understand; it's about trusting God with the details of my life. Either he is who he says he is, or God is a liar. So I guess I'll dig in this dirt and see if he pulls out any gold.

Yes, I'm mad as hell, but I refuse to allow hell

to drive me mad.

Alissa

Chapter 1: *Promise*

I broke a promise to my girls yesterday. Yup, it wasn't my first offense, and it probably won't be my last. Don't count me out as a bad Mom though. Making slime wasn't on my list of top priorities for the day. Although the kids cleaned their rooms and straightened up their toys, just like they had promised me, I failed in making sure my promise of messy slime-making would be on the agenda for the evening.

From the time we're old enough to learn how to tie a promise with our pinky and seal it with a kiss, it becomes one of the most basic life lessons we learn as children. I'll never forget the first time my daughter looked at me with crocodile tears and puppy dog eyes as she said, "But Mommy ... you promised! You aren't allowed to break a promise, right?

Pretzel ties and strawberry kisses make it FOREVER."

Of course, not everyone has fancy names like pretzel ties and strawberry kisses as they lock pinkies and kiss their hand, but we do because promises are special to us. Yet somehow, I still manage to break some.

It's funny isn't it? As we get older, the line for "I promise" becomes blurred. What used to be sealed within a pretzel tie and strawberry kiss, all of a sudden becomes sealed with nothing more than good intentions, bribes, and wishful thinking, knowing there's no true guarantee it will ever take place. Growing up has a way of changing us, and somehow non-negotiables (like breaking a promise) become our reality in life.

I suppose that even in our church-going, faith-building, Bible-declaring lifestyles, that's why promise is so hard to count on. Is there really any guarantee, or is it all just wishful thinking? I mean let's be real. Life changes, circumstances shift, tragedies happen, goals aren't met, people change ... and who knows what tomorrow may hold? Does that uncertainty in life alter God's promise for us? Is it all just a reward system for good behavior, convenience, and perfect lifestyles? Or is it something that's truly available no matter what because ... hey, it's a promise.

I'm going to pause real quick and apologize while we're ahead of the game, just in case you've picked up this book and aren't a consistent churchgoer. My Pentecostal upbringing likes to speak out sometimes, and I automatically assume that everybody was raised in a tongue-talking, fire-falling, hair-flying, pulpit-slapping atmosphere. If that's not you, please know I admire you.

Yes, you read that right. I admire you! You got to see life from a much different perspective than I did, and for that you should be eternally grateful. (Cue the weird, little, alien guys from Toy Story as I say that, from the bottom of my heart to yours.) Now before anything is taken out of context and someone gets the idea that I'm bad-mouthing the place that made me the strong woman I am today, please let me explain.

More times than not, I've heard promise echo through the church as pastors delivered their best sermons in hopes of helping us to hold on and keep pushing toward the goal. I don't know about you, but I found myself scratching my head and asking, *How much holding on does one person have to do before they finally see the promise become reality? Is it ever really a thing or are we just hopeful and ignorant in our belief system?*

My arsenal of "Promise Land" messages are too many to count. With songs, book titles, and revival slogans, those sermons have been all the rage for more years than I am old. Unfortunately, like many in my nearly thirty years of churchgoing, I've seen more people *pushing* toward promise than I've ever seen *possessing* the promise. And over the years, I found I wasn't the only one who had become discouraged in this area time and time again.

Promise, to me, was nothing more than a mind-numbing message that the church had on repeat. It had become a good sermon, a positive song, and a whole lot of word vomit that I'd learned to regurgitate from the many pastors before me when life made no sense at all. I would say things like, "Hold on to the promise and stay faithful!" even when I wanted to quit, or, "His promises are yes and amen!" even when I felt like life was screaming, "NO!" over and over again. I guess you could say *promise* was something I'd become desensitized to because it wasn't something I'd truly experienced, on a consistent basis, outside of all the hype within the church walls.

Now don't get me wrong, I'm not saying I haven't seen God move mountains, answer prayers, and prove his faithfulness ... because I have. In fact, I have a lifetime of journals filled with pages of personal stories that prove he's all the things he says he is in his Word. (I'm even sharing some of those entries with you throughout this book.) What I *am* saying is that, more times than not, *promise* was a place I found myself wandering in the wilderness to find, rather than a place I truly lived in.

To me, promise had become painful and didn't bring me purpose. It reminded me of the Israelites who died without knowing what promise truly felt like.

Confession #1: For so long, I felt like I had a life full of dreams but no destinations. *Promise* was a joke to me.

Maybe you've been there. Maybe you haven't. Either way, I admire those of you who haven't had the opportunity to become numb, in one way or another, to the idea of promise. I truly look up to those who haven't had to resensitize their mind to the truth of what promise truly is and to those who haven't been worn down by familiar messages that don't bring freedom to your life.

If that's you, then you've truly lived. And I applaud you.

Unfortunately, many of us are having to retrain our mind to understand that promises are meant to be kept and not broken. We're having to remind ourselves that *promise* is worth feeling, *promise* is true, and *promise* can be ours.

The year 2017 was unique for me because it took me through a process I never expected to take. It was heart wrenching. It was terrifying. It was empowering. It was destructive. It was refreshing. But most of all, it was everything I never thought promise would entail.

Through it all, I discovered the truth about that word. That word we're so unsure of. That word whose meaning changes between childhood and adulthood. That word that carries such depth and rings from the pulpits of churches across the world. And I want to share that truth with you because it's simple, really—but it just might blow your mind.

Are you ready? Repeat after me …

Promise has absolutely nothing to do with anyone else, but it has everything to do with me.

Let me share with you some history about myself that led me to the place I'm at now in life. I didn't know it at the time, but 2017 would be the year that marked my understanding of what promise really looked like. That was the word that would start my year off strong and give me hope by breathing fresh air into my lungs.

New Year's Day started out just as it always does for me. I led worship for my parents' church by ushering in one of those good-ole Pentecostal experiences. In case you haven't been involved in one of those, it includes dancing, shouting, pulpit-slapping, and worshipping God until you sweat your makeup off. So we rang in the new year by praising God for what he was going to do in 2017 and thanking him for what he had brought us through in the year before. Promise rang from the pulpit, and we were encouraged to push toward the goal once more.

And I kid you not, I remember dreading the whole thing. My mind wasn't in the game, and to be completely honest, church was the last place I wanted to be that night. I remember the conversation I had with my then-husband. I didn't want to go to service at all that day. In fact, I complained, looked for ways out of it, and made excuses to not go. Truth be told, I was upset at the fact that I had to lead worship that night; I knew it would require me to mask my face with filtered joy, since 2016 was a year of pure chaos for our family.

If you're reading this book, then I can bet money that you've felt the effects of wreckage, at one point or another, in your life. To clarify what I mean by "wreckage," I'm not talking about slip-ups or little mistakes here and there. The kind of wreckage I'm talking about is the kind that makes your head spin so fast that you're not quite sure of who you are or how you got there.

That's where we were at during that time in our life. Life as we knew it had been flipped upside down, and everything we considered normal had become completely void of existence. Transition was how we started

2016 off, by deciding to move our family from Texas to Arkansas. With ministry having been the core of our life for so long, we felt that God was calling us to take a slower pace than we were used to. So we closed a significant chapter in our life and started fresh, with family being our main goal.

Texas, to us, was not only known as God's country, but it was also known as home. We had a beautiful house whose backyard came with the picture-perfect, childhood tree with a rope swing attached. Our lives were full of routine, and great jobs that came with just about every benefit we could ever want. We'd pastored a growing and thriving church for nearly seven years alongside my parents, and we were surrounded by family and friends. Our biggest accomplishments while we were planted there were the two little heartbeats that joined our world; Kinsleigh Reign and Aurora Danielle are the biggest blessings a mother could have ever prayed for. So, as you can imagine, Texas was full of memories, ministry, loving people, traveling, writing music, and living our best life. Well, at least we *thought* we were. But the reality was much the opposite.

The truth is, my ex-husband and I never had a strong marriage. In Texas we could easily cover it up by staying busy and making sure our agendas were full of ministry and loving our kids. When we had fallouts, we pushed through, kept existing, and made it work the best we could … for our girls' sake. But once the decision was made to leave and pursue this new season of our life, we found that our busy schedule became nonexistent … which means it became even more difficult to keep covering up our problems.

Let me tell you, something happens to the whole dynamic of your relationship when you go from having your own home and good money, to moving in with five other people and barely being able to make ends meet. It was exhausting. It was confusing. It left us questioning where God was, and why we weren't seeing progress when *he* was the one who had led us to move. *Did we make a mistake? Should we have left a ministry that was thriving and doing well?* Questions that became constant in our life were, "How are we going to make it to tomorrow?" and "God led us in this direction, so where is he?"

So the thought of leading worship on that last night of 2016 brought me more frustration than freedom. It left me reflecting over our decisions and questioning the future. Friends, the new year was calling my name, loud and clear, and I was ready for it. I was tired of struggling, tired of having no money, tired of being homeless, and tired of feeling like my life consisted of no purpose.

Regardless, I spent the last hours and minutes of the year leading worship, not realizing that in that moment I'd receive a word that would keep me through the darkest season of my life. It was in that moment—that I'd fought so hard to not be a part of—where I would be given a pretzel tie and strawberry kiss from the Father. And oh, how I would cling to it for dear life.

That moment would be my reminder to God, through my crocodile tears over the next year, saying, "This makes it forever!" For it was in that moment that my entire view of promise would begin to take shape. I had no idea how significant it would be for my future, but the mark would be grand.

Confession

For so long, my life was full of dreams but no destinations. *Promise* was a joke.

Truth

Promise has nothing to do with anyone else but has everything to do with me.

Journal entry
June 17, 2017

Hello,

The hole is big, and the shovel is heavy. I feel like my husband has dug us into the biggest mess possible, and I'm not sure how we'll get out.

Today, my ears heard the saddest thing I think they've ever heard: "My daddy moved out of our house. He isn't our daddy anymore ... I don't know why he left us."

I thought I might puke while listening to my five-year-old have a discussion with her friend as we sat on a bench eating snow cones after a sunny pool day. Her friend's grandma shot her eyes at me with concern, but I didn't give any details. All I could do was brush the hair out of Rory's face while gently saying, "Baby, it's ok. Daddy is still your daddy ... we will get through this. I promise."

It's only been about a week since he looked our baby girls in the eyes and told them he was moving out. I think my brain has been seared with the memory of that night forever. And I'm pretty positive that my seven-year-old's words, as she stood in the doorway and watched her daddy drive away, will forever haunt me, "Mommy, there used to be four of us, but now there's only three. Will I have to grow up without a daddy at home forever?"

We all cried ourselves to sleep that night ...

Today was the first day I've had to handle the kids talking about it outside of our home. I can't blame them. I can't stop them. Their little hearts are hurting just as bad as mine, but I think the worst part is that I can't relate to them. My dad never left me, but my husband has. It's two totally different types of abandonment.

How do I help them heal?

I can sit and think of all the things I don't quite understand, but what I've learned the most throughout this nightmare is that life is full of opportunity.

So now I choose me. I choose my kids. I choose to not focus on the what-ifs of life. I choose to begin to pour myself into the knowledge of who I am in Christ and what he has for my life and my daughters'.

My last entry ended with me saying I'm going to dig in the dirt to find the gold that's waiting for us. I'll leave this entry by recalling a childhood memory of mine. I was digging in the garden with my great-grandma, and her words hold truer now than ever before, "If you don't get dirty when you dig, then you aren't doing it right. Before anything can grow you have to be willing to do the work."

I guess this is where the work begins for us … but I remain confident that we *will* see growth from it.

Alissa

Chapter 2: Dig

I don't know if you've ever experienced it before—the quiet
hush that falls over a room when God's presence is heavy within it. All
you can do is sit in awe while a tangible love sweeps through the
atmosphere, bringing instantaneous peace to every area of your heart. I
remember that love causing me to fall to my knees during worship on
New Year's Eve night with tears running down my face. I laid all my
frustrations, questions, doubt, and anger out on the stage as I sang a
spontaneous song of hope over the people. And while doing so,
something in my spirit leapt as I felt the Lord say something simple but
true, *This is your year of dreams come true. Everything I've ever
promised you is yours. Even when the clock strikes midnight, remember*

that it's in the midnight hour where I turn it around.

I can't explain how, but I've never been surer of a word from God than I was in that moment of life. At 11:57 p.m. on the last day of 2016, kneeling on the ground with mascara running down my face, I had hope.

Little did I know, God was preparing me for the clock to strike midnight, and promise would be a process I'd have to walk out. I had no idea at that time, but over the next year of my life I would become painfully aware of the fact that promise is a posture and not a position.

po ·si ·tion[1]

pə ˈzi-shən

noun

1. A place where someone or something is located or has been put
2. A particular way in which someone or something is placed or arranged

pos ·ture[2]

ˈpäs-chər

noun

1. The position in which someone holds their body when standing or siting
2. A particular way of dealing with or considering something; an approach or attitude

Listen, what if I told you that anyone can steal your position from you, but no one can keep you from posturing yourself correctly? *Promise* is yours as long as you choose it. It's not something you can lose, and it's not something that can be stolen from you. Your promise, destiny, dream, calling, vision—whatever you choose to name it—is 100 percent dependent upon your ability to posture yourself correctly and move toward that goal.

A friend once said, "You'll always remain in the same place if you never take a step forward." I've found that the same concept can be applied here, too. Digging requires a certain amount of work, strength, consistency, and endurance, but the one thing weighing heavily toward its success is your posture. You can dig until your hands form blisters and sweat soaks through your shirt, but if you haven't maintained the right posture, you won't last long. It may not seem like a big deal to you, but if it's not a priority then it'll become your pain.

My great-grandparents were farmers, and one of the lessons I remember my grandma teaching me was the importance behind how you hold a shovel and what your posture looks like. I can still hear her words, "If you dig wrong, then you'll wear out fast." What I learned, the hard way, was that correct posture not only helps your endurance, but it also keeps you from injuring what allows you to get the job done—and that, my friend, is your back.

I don't know where you're at in life right now, and I don't know why you picked up this book. Maybe you've had wreckage around you for a long time. Maybe you're just now seeing the effects of chaos in your life. Or maybe you've lived with it for so long that you don't even recognize it anymore. Wherever you are, I want you to understand today that promise is yours. But to find the gold, you have to be willing to dig through the dirt behind the pain.

During 2017, I learned what it meant to position myself toward that process. I had to accept that my promise had nothing to do with the pain in my life, the people who caused it, the God who seemed to have forgotten me, or the cruel hand life seemed to have dealt me. It did, however, have everything to do with how I chose to posture myself while I had that shovel in my hand.

Sure, there were all kinds of ways I wanted to use that shovel in the heat of the moment.

Let's be real, when you're mad as hell, all you want is revenge for your broken heart. But what I had to realize was that the only thing that was going to get me out of that mess was to dig my way out. No one was going to do it for me, and no one was going to make me do it myself. I had to choose.

Throughout my years of working in the ministry, I've seen all kinds of tragedy and all kinds of pain. I've seen wreckage mark the lives of innocent people with suicide, abuse, molestation, rape, murder, and loss. Over time, as I helped them sort through the pieces of their life, I tried to make sense of the pain they felt. But one thing never seemed to add up. *If God is so good then how come some people strike gold in recovery and move on in life, while others find a mudslide waiting for them on the other side of the mountain and stay forever stuck?*

It wasn't until 2017, when I found myself confronting my own battle, that I realized *promise* has nothing to do with circumstance, situations, or the people involved. It does, however, have everything to do with the decision to properly position yourself toward the promise. That's what will determine the outcome of your life, and how you'll allow tragedy to mark your story. This is one of the hardest revelations you'll ever have to accept in life, because it requires you to take ownership of your outcome, even when you weren't in control of the thing that got you there in the first place.

If you never read another page of this book, the biggest thing I want you to walk away knowing is that *promise* is yours, but *posture* must be a priority. I'm going to say something cliché here, but it's truth, so hear me out. God did not give you a backbone so you could replace it with a wishbone.

God did not give you a backbone so you could

replace it with a wishbone.

Please don't injure the thing that's going to take you from a position of pushing (longing, desiring, and wanting something) to a posture of possessing (owning, controlling, and dominating) the promise for your life. Wishing it all away, no matter how hard you try, won't get you anywhere when it comes to your destiny. Digging is going to require work, strength, and endurance.

You are the answer to the restoration in your life because Jesus can't fix what you don't allow him to touch.

So I want to ask you, When are you going to make the decision to posture your heart differently? When are you going to stop marching, with your shovel held high for revenge, toward the ones who hurt you? When are you going to stop punishing yourself by burying your pain and refusing to deal with the issues? When are you going to lower the shovel of shame you've been holding over your head for so long?

Friend, when are you going to start digging so you can find the gold waiting on the other side of your grief, guilt, and all the garbage that's been holding you back from your promise?

Before we can go any further in this book, let me shake these pages for you and say this: Get up off the ground and posture yourself toward promise correctly! Find some backbone and dig! No one else can do it for you, and no one else can be the answer you need to move forward. You're the one who decides where you go from here. So what will it be?

I can confidently say from experience, I know it hurts. … I know you don't understand it all. I know you're mad as hell. I know you want revenge, answers, and for it all to be over. And do you know what? That's okay! You're allowed to be all those things. You're allowed to feel all those things. You're allowed to go through days where you can't get out of bed. You're allowed to have moments where you can't seem to look at yourself in the mirror. You're allowed to experience bad seasons in your life. And in case no one's told you lately, let me remind you of the fact that God isn't mad at you for any of this! In fact, I'll let you in on a secret: He isn't even disappointed in you.

Confession #2: I wasted years of my life wandering around in the wilderness, numb to the truth of promise.

I was shackled to the idea that promise was on the way as long as I kept pressing forward and wishing I could find it. The problem was that pressing forward always seemed to be tied to keeping a list of rules, regulations, and standards within the church. It kept me bound to disappointment as I found myself taking two steps forward and ten steps back. It left me in a state of hopelessness as the church continued to scream, "Keep pressing. Keep trying. Keep doing all you can do. … You will get there one day."

But one day I decided that "one day" wasn't good enough for me.

One thing my kids remind me of every time a promise is made is that "I promise" means now, not later. Why is it that we're taught a different mindset within the church? Why is it that we're so brainwashed into thinking our promise is connected to the possibility of "one day"? Why have we replaced promise and the hope we have in Christ with the expectation of brokenness?

Didn't the Father say he knows the plans he has for me? Didn't he say his plans are to prosper me and not to harm me? I'm pretty sure he even said, in Jeremiah 29:11, that they're plans to give me hope and a future, right?

Hear me loud and clear, y'all. Any message that does not bring hope, does not bring Christ. Your promise is not a possibility. Your promise is a *guarantee*! It's here and it's yours ... if you choose it. So please—for the love of coffee—stop believing the lie that pressing forward requires perfection! The Father never asked you to be perfect. He simply asked you to be present in the process. Moving forward cannot be accomplished by remaining in the same place. Moving forward requires action!

Any message that does not bring hope, does not bring Christ.

Your promise isn't on the way. It's right under your feet. You simply must learn to dig!

With that being said, I want you to understand that you're allowed to feel the depths of every emotion while navigating through this season of your life. What you're not allowed to do, is give hell the opportunity to drive you mad while you're walking through it. How you choose to position yourself is the deciding factor for whether you'll wander in the wilderness or feel the ground of promise underneath your feet.

God's ability to keep his vow to you has nothing to do with anyone else. It has nothing to do with what they've put you through, or the mark they've left on your heart. His word has absolutely everything to do with you! You are the one who determines whether you're willing to see promise become a destination in your life or remain a dream. You are the answer, not the issue. So start digging.

Before you move on from here, ask yourself, Am I willing to feel promise again?

If your answer is yes, then you've got to get up and dig! Put down the pills, pour out the alcohol, sever the relationships in your life that are holding you back, and stop scrolling through social media pages that are keeping you tied to your past. Stop longing for the brass life you left behind when God has a future full of gold waiting up ahead. Let's find it together! I promise you it's there. The moment he shaped you and said, "It is good," was the moment he sealed your forever with a kiss. God cannot break his Word, and even if he could, he isn't going to start with you. I never said this would be easy, and I never said God would do all the work. But what I will say is that it's worth every bit of blood, sweat, and tears you'll put into it as you sort through the wreckage.

I used to hear my Grandpa shout from the pulpit, "God will pull you through if you can stand the pull!" but I'm here to shout from these pages that there's gold waiting for you if you can stand long enough to dig! I promise.

Confession

I wasted years of my life wandering around in the wilderness, numb
to the truth of promise.

Truth

Promise is a posture, not a position.

Journal entry

June 18, 2017

Hello,

Another day, another obstacle, another journey to figure out how to get through. I'm desperately grasping for any little bit of air I can find. I'm holding on to acceptance like "It's mine!" because the truth is that rejection is all I know at the moment. I need some hope.

I never knew I could feel pain like this. Anxiety rises daily, and I feel like life is a miss. How did I get here? Where did I go wrong and why can't I breathe? My body feels as though it's rejecting the very air in its lungs, and I'm finding it hard to find the will to even live for my girls.

I'm in a constant state of sickness. My stomach feels like it's eating itself, and I could swear I ate rocks because I feel them tearing my insides apart. My head is constantly swimming with thoughts, fear, questions, and confusion. My heart feels like it's attacking every beat it's trying to pump, and it leaves my chest with a constant ache. Is it possible that my body doesn't even know how to function through this?

I wouldn't doubt it ...

This man said he loved me. ... He said he would love me forever. Then what? He just decides to leave after ten years of marriage and two beautiful baby girls? Was my heart nothing more than a joke to him? Was my love really that forgettable? Was our life really that worthless? Was our family really that trashable?

Right now, life isn't easy. Probably the hardest it's ever been. But I cling to the faithful love of the Father like it's the last breath in my body. I've never been so angry and confused in my entire life. How someone stops loving you after nearly ten years of marriage is beyond me. How someone can walk out on their family and want to be alone living a new life is something I can't comprehend.

But this one thing I do know is that I refuse to let this destroy me. Today, I choose me. I choose to work on me. If I take anything away from this, I choose to take away the fact that I'm going to use this opportunity to become the woman, mother, and leader I was always meant to be. This will not staunch me ... it will launch me.

This will not staunch me ... it will launch me.

Staunch means to stop the flow, and I will not allow divorce, rejection, hurt, and abandonment to create an atmosphere of bitterness in my heart. I'll allow it to force me to work extra hard to create an

29

atmosphere for making my heart better.

Today is Father's Day. I'm presented with an opportunity to show him just how bad he hurt me last month when he didn't give me so much as a "Happy Mother's Day." My kids had to ask my mom to go get gifts for me because their dad wouldn't do it, and it just broke my heart. I will never forget that day. I felt so rejected … not as a wife, but as the mother of his children. You know what? I think that almost cut me worse than anything at all.

The opportunity to show rejection and pain toward him today is real. But I won't.

Instead, I woke up as angry as a bull, and sat down with the cards and gifts I bought for him. As I was getting them ready, I realized this Father's Day is different than the years before. This time I'm not celebrating a loving father and husband. Instead, I'm celebrating a man who left us and won't give us an explanation as to why or for whom.

I find myself asking, Will I allow this to push me back or bump me forward in my relationship, call, integrity, and love for the Father?

As painful as it is … I choose forward.

I wrote him a note about how great of a father I've known him to be in the past. I let him know that the kids see him as their moon and stars, and I encouraged him to never stop shining for them.

I told him that I love and miss him dearly, and you know what? It was hard—gut-punching and teeth-grinding kind of hard. I'm still mad as hell, but once again I refuse to allow hell to drive me mad. Heaven can't come down when hell has a place in my environment.

My husband has a lot going on, even if he won't admit it.

Emotionally, mentally, spiritually. His heart is a mess and he feels it. There's a whole lot he's not telling me. I feel it deep down in my spirit. Lies are being covered up, and he's dealt with all of this differently than I would have.

So I'll pray. Stand in the gap. Love him through my pain. Move forward and let beauty grow from something impossible.

So … Happy Father's Day, God. You are the best daddy. The place I sing to, run to, hope in, heal in, love, cherish, and fight to never lose.

I'm leaving for several weeks. I'm going to stay with family in Kansas. I need some distraction. I need time to find direction for my marriage. And honestly, my kids need some joy right now.

Life is not always what you expect, but it doesn't have to be what you accept either.

I don't accept this for my life. I don't accept that separation, or even the possibility of divorce, is greater than the name of Jesus. I'm broken-hearted but I know the mender. Whatever the outcome … I know he will be faithful.

Life is not what you always expect, but it doesn't have to be what you accept either.

Alissa

Chapter 3: *Dirt*

I don't know if you're aware of this, but there has to be one component involved in order to dig … and that's dirt.

I'll never forget the day that dirt became valuable to me. I'd found myself sitting on an old, wooden church pew, tucked away on my back porch, as I tried to catch my breath. Emotionally broken and escaping the questions of "Where is daddy?" I sat there helpless as life seemed to be disintegrating right before my eyes. I don't know how it always seems to happen; I suppose it could be the fact that I'm a creative, and my heart is always searching for beauty in the most impossible ways. But regardless, there it was. A picture of hope, in the shape of a broken flowerpot, resting at my feet.

I remember planting those flowers with my girls that spring. They were so excited to pick them out and chose just about every color so they could create the entire rainbow. When we arrived home, we spent our entire afternoon getting our hands dirty, soaking up the sun, and eating cold watermelon while we watched the sun set.

It made me incredibly sad to now see that beautiful memory broken and void of life. What once was full of color, was now nothing more than a mushed-up mess of dirt and death, with roots lying on the surface of what used to give them stability and a place to call home.

Ironic isn't it? That seemed to be a picture of my life in more ways than one.

I can't recall the amount of times a church pew has reminded me of the dirt in my life, but I suppose if I tried to count them all, it would look much like a permanent body cast molded into the wood and would remind me of where my place was in life.

Yet still I kept coming back to claim my spot.

If church people could be given any award, it would be for claiming seats that aren't theirs, but this one seemed to be made for me. Besides the fact that I was a perfect fit, I'm pretty sure you could find my name engraved within the grain.

Those flowers seemed so familiar to me, and that church pew felt much like home. What used to be full, vibrant, and flourishing now looked like nothing more than a pile of dirt and broken pieces laying at my feet. It only seemed natural for me to find my place on a seat that looked much like all the others had during the darkest times of my life. The only problem was that this place never brought me answers; it only ever brought me shame.

Confession #3: I'm tired of feeling like I have to cover up the dirt

in my life … Instead, I'm learning to embrace it.

Something happens when you're left uprooted and unfiltered. Every ounce of your identity feels exposed, and suddenly you can feel in ways you never had the ability to feel before. With nothing to cover up the pain, mistakes, and filth of life, you begin to realize that the only thing left to do is to embrace it and move forward.

So that's what I did.

I sat on that pew and stared at the picture of my life that rested on the ground in the shape of a broken flowerpot. It was piled with dirt and exposed roots but hope suddenly began to rise up from the depths of my soul. I don't know how it happened, but that was the moment that marked my understanding forever.

Dirt doesn't make me dirty. In fact, there is promise hidden within it.

Dirt doesn't make me dirty. In fact, there is promise

hidden within it.

Have you ever felt like you were being uprooted against your will?

Like everything you'd ever planted in life was being ripped from the ground you'd faithfully tended to and cared for? Maybe it was a business idea you poured your heart and soul into only to see it flop. Maybe it was your child whom you faithfully raised in church and, without warning, they confessed that they don't believe in your God. Maybe it was your health, and despite doing every little thing right, you were diagnosed with an illness you couldn't control. Maybe it was an unexpected loss in your life that you weren't ready for.

Whatever it was, I'm right there with you.

I felt as though everything I'd planted in life, and spent years nurturing and cultivating, had been forcefully ripped from the ground it called home. Every root that was labeled—family, provision, protection, faith, ministry, love, trust, covenant—was desperately clinging to any bit of dirt it could find to help bring back the life it was losing.

The church has done a great job at teaching me all about plastic joy, and how to rotate masks on a daily basis. But it's done a horrible job of teaching me how to find freedom beyond the filtered life, and because of that, I sat in bondage to wrong mindsets for far too long.

It wasn't until I was twenty-seven years old that I found myself looking in the mirror and unable to recognize the green eyes looking back at me. *How did I get here? Who is this woman I've become? Why are her eyes so full of sorrow? And most importantly, who has taken her smile?* She didn't know who she was anymore, and worse than that, she didn't even know how her life had gotten to where it was.

I remember an old home video of me when I was only seven years old. My eyes sparkled with green and blue hues of confidence, and my dirty-blonde waves bounced from the joy found in my feet. I pranced through the living room wearing an old, raggedy blanket tied around my shoulders, and proudly held a broomstick in my hand. It never once crossed my mind how silly I must have looked. As far as my seven-year-old self was concerned, I was Queen Alissa! I saw that old blanket as a floor-length robe lined in satin and shining with emeralds to match my eyes. That nasty ol' broomstick was a golden scepter covered in rubies and topped with a diamond so big it could be seen from miles away.

There was absolutely zero shame. There was undeniably no guilt. And more than either of those things … there was no dirt to be covered up. I was Alissa, and I was proud to be her.

But I lost her to shame somewhere along the way and covered her up with fake freedom found at the altar. I was taught that dirt makes me dirty, and the blood of Jesus makes me clean. So I never fully understood that being clean doesn't mean dirt never marked me.

Now I know different.

Being clean simply means I no longer have to allow dirt to define my life, because the blood of Jesus is enough.

My husband, Brandon, says it so beautifully, "You are not dirty and distant. You are clean and close."

You are not dirty and distant. You are clean and close.

What if I told you the dirt in your life doesn't distract God from seeing the purpose inside you? In fact, dirt is what he molded you from.

Just picture it: a God who's without one single flaw, getting down on his hands and knees to form and mold relationship from the dust of the ground. I can only imagine what the angels thought that day as they looked down from Heaven to see God, in all his glory, sitting in a pile of mud with dirt under his fingernails and filth on his hands. Even more surprising than that, I wonder what their reaction was when they realized he was creating life that would reflect his image. How is that possible? What was he thinking? Didn't he realize how crazy that must have seemed?

Oftentimes, we disqualify ourselves from our purpose, call, anointing, gifts, talents, and destiny because of the dirt we see around us. We take our place, with a church-pew-view, and look for ways to cover up the mess. And I like to believe that God sits back and laughs, knowing that dirt was the thing that qualified us from the beginning of time. From the moment he kissed our filth and breathed his life into our lungs, he stood with traces of our dirt left on his hands, saying, "It is good."

The more I think of it, the more I realize how intentional he is in all that he does. Why did he choose dirt to create us? Why did he choose to design us in his image with the dirtiest thing he could find? I truly believe it's because he wanted to prove to us that being clean was never the qualifier for his love, acceptance, and destiny for our life. In fact, dirt is what made him choose us in the first place. He saw destiny in your dirt before it ever had the chance to become clean.

He saw destiny in your dirt before it ever had the

chance to become clean.

As I sat looking at that broken pot, I saw promise within the dirt. Among the mess of exposed roots, I noticed there was one lonely, purple flower blooming amidst it all. That one flower reminded me of promise once more as it pushed through the disruption of life and refused to die. Even in the midst of chaos, that one flower was saying, "No matter what the circumstances are—yes, even if my roots have been ripped up and exposed—I refuse to accept this as my destiny! I will choose to grow through the impossible!"

So many times, we're told to "grow through what we go through." But, friend, I'm here to tell you that you're not the thing that grows through the chaos of life. No, you are more than that. You're the soil that determines how the seeds of your life will grow. Your promise has nothing to do with anyone else but has everything to do with you. Your life is the fertile ground that gives place for seeds to take root and manifest around you. How do you see yourself, and what do you believe about your situation? Your beliefs will set the atmosphere for those seeds to grow.

You are not dirty ... there is destiny written there.

You are not dirty ... there is destiny written there.

For so long, I found myself trying to be everything the church said I needed to be in order to be labeled "clean." I was filtered with fake smiles, laughs, and encouraging words when, deep down inside, I was screaming for someone to see the real me before I lost my ever-loving mind trying to be someone I wasn't. I had this "churchy" ability to mask all my flaws by covering up what was really beneath the surface of my filtered life.

Religion has a way of training some of the fakest people you will ever meet, and although I wasn't fake in my love for Jesus, I did struggle with truly knowing his love for me.

Why do we feel the need to be someone we're not? Why do we feel like life is all about meeting the expectation of what others' idea of acceptable is, at the expense of our own personal acceptance? I mean, come on, they have weeds in their garden just as much as I do.

Searching for the acceptance found in church has almost killed me, too many times than I'd like to admit. Religion has a way of doing that. It even came to kill Jesus.

My first thought when my life began to crumble around me was, *How can I cover this up? How can I make this look less messy so that others don't lose their view of who I am?* In hindsight this makes me laugh, because the truth is … divorce is messy. There's no "covering up" the side effects of what it looks like in your life. Everyone around you will see it, so no one even has to bring it up. That became crystal clear to me when I received my first private message on Facebook concerning the matter.

> Hey Alissa. I haven't seen your husband in any of your
>
> photos or posts lately. Are y'all doing ok? It's not like you to
>
> not include him on your page in some way or another.

News flash! People notice dirt. (No, let me rephrase that.) People look for dirt—specifically yours.

That was my first private message on social media, but I soon found out that it wouldn't be my last.

No decision had yet been made concerning the outcome of my marriage. I was standing in the gap and believing that God was going to restore all the wreckage, and that my husband was going to return home. The thought that people were already making pre-conceived ideas of what was going on in my life (before I fully knew the depths of it myself) made me sick to my stomach, and I found myself looking for ways to cover the dirt before I became labeled as "dirty." That was until I realized something significant …

A person is only as good as their dirt.

Sounds crazy right? I thought so too, until I began to study Genesis. Let's read:

And the Lord God formed man of the dust of the ground, and breathed into his nostrils the breath of life; and man became a living being. (Genesis 2:7, NKJV)

In case no one else ever tells you this, let me be the one to shine some light on the dark areas of your heart. … Dirt is not the division of your relationship with Christ. It is the detail that formed the relationship in the first place.

If I could help you look at creation from a different perspective, I'd ask you to think of a world without dirt. Would that mean there would be no *us?*

In the church, we've been taught that we were clean from the beginning, and sin is what made us dirty. But it's my belief that we were always dirty, and sin is what opened our eyes to see the reality of who we truly are. It never defined the love that the Father had for us; it was just a part of who we were. Could it be that from the beginning of time, the dirt in our life has never been the focus? Have we got it all wrong when it comes to what makes us acceptable in the Father's eyes?

I believe we've majored on minors within the church because the reality is that it's never been about us. It's always been about him. He chose us from the moment he formed us from the ground. He shaped our purpose and gave us life, knowing we could never maintain cleanliness on our own.

So many times, we put limitations on a limitless God and then wonder why we never seem to move forward. We shackle ourselves to some dirty moment in our timeline and allow it to define us for the rest of our days. But the Father's heart was never to bring us filters to cover up our filth. He set the precedent from the beginning by showing us there's freedom in the understanding of who he created us to be.

Who is that exactly? It's simple … we are his.

The ability to be labeled as "clean" isn't found within yourself. It's found within the understanding that, even when you're covered in dirt, you're constantly being perfected by the one who holds your heart and keeps you in the palm of his hand. His grace is sufficient, and his love never fails. And I find it interesting that, despite our dirt, the Father gave us authority to rule and reign over every area of our life. He even went as far as to bless it by saying, "Be fruitful and multiply." (see Genesis 1:26-28, NKJV)

How many times do we use the excuse that God could never bless our mess? How many times do we think nothing good can grow from the dirt found within our life? How many times do we sit down in shame, not realizing we're the soil that can help produce growth in our life?

Listen, it's never been about your ability to stay clean. It's always been about your ability to grow through the impossible by allowing him to be the determining factor in your life. You can't do it without him, and although he can do it without you, he chose to partner with you in life.

Sitting in my living room, on Father's Day morning of 2017, was probably the first time I was presented with an opportunity to show the Father my heart's willingness to grow through the impossible. I had to decide to not allow my pain to become my position in life, and to allow purpose to become my posture.

Something I found to be true is that when you dig through the dirt of your life, you'll find weeds that need pulled, roots beginning to lay exposed, and rocks that were hiding. And it wasn't easy; it was painful, messy, and time consuming. What I had to remember was that God was taking me through a process toward *promise*, and that was the place where true growth was found, in the midst of the impossible.

I sat on my porch one day, feeling the weight of life and the struggle to breathe. I was looking for ways to cover up my dirt, but what I found was the hope of promise hidden within it all. And I realized, in an instant, that God doesn't want me any other way. He chose to take me as I am … unapologetically me and unfiltered.

Today, I want you to find the same answer for yourself. No matter how bad you've been tumbled around, no matter how much fullness you've lost, no matter how bad your roots have been damaged, I want you to know there's still a chance for you to bloom through the

#UNFILTERED

impossible. You can still say, "I refuse this as my destiny! Life may not be what I expected, but this will not be what I accept!"

> Planted in the house of the Lord,
>
> they will flourish in the courts of our God. (Psalm 92:13)

One thing that gave my heart hope during that season of my life was the promise found within my name. Have you ever thought about the fact that, even though the Father created all of creation from the dust of the ground, the only thing he personally took time to name was mankind?

You may feel like your identity has been stolen from you, lost within your past (without hope for a future), but I want you to know, today, that he has called you by name even when he didn't have to. You are clean and close to his heart, and no amount of dirt can make you distant enough for him to leave you nameless.

Let me gently ask you something I had to ask myself. How are the filters in your life working out for you? Are they treating your heart well or are they damaging you more? For me, I found that the filters weren't covering me ... they were killing me. I found that my identity was getting lost within them, and they were beginning to steal my name. My heart was being poisoned by unrealistic expectations, and I wasn't finding purpose in the acceptance of Jesus and his love anymore. I thought covering my wreckage was the answer, but it was canceling out my authority to walk in who I was created to be.

44

Could it be that what separated Adam and Eve from the Father wasn't sin itself? Could it be that, the moment they began to filter the truth about who they truly were, they blocked their ability to accept the Father for who he truly is? Could it be that covering their wreckage canceled their authority to walk in their design?

Then the eyes of both of them were opened, and they realized they were naked; so they sewed fig leaves together and made coverings for themselves.

Then the man and his wife heard the sound of the LORD God as he was walking in the garden in the cool of the day, and they hid from the LORD God among the trees of the garden. But the LORD God called to the man, "Where are you?"

He answered, "I heard you in the garden, and I was afraid because I was naked; so I hid."

And he said, "Who told you that you were naked? Have you eaten from the tree that I commanded you not to eat from?"

(Genesis 3:8-11)

Our knee-jerk reaction in life is to filter our sin by covering up our dirt.

Adam and Eve were the first humans to ever put on a filter that wasn't theirs to wear. It may not have been as cute as Snapchat's puppy-dog faces and butterfly crowns, but it was enough to make them unrecognizable.

Sin has a way of opening our eyes to the fact that we are a spirit-man wrapped up in flesh. Yet somehow, despite the imperfections within our life, God still replies, *Who told you that you were naked*?

When restoration found its way back into my life, I had the honor of getting remarried, and he's the man of my dreams. But one night as I sat in our living room, my thoughts became flooded with the lie that I'll never be the wife Brandon needs me to be. The pain of watching my ex-husband walk away held me captive to seeing myself through the lens of rejection, and gave me the idea that, no matter what I do, I'll eventually be left again.

Brandon's response healed my heart in more ways than he could ever know. "Who told you that? Who told you that you weren't enough? Who told you that you aren't lovable? Who told you that you're rejected? That isn't what God said! He said that you're exactly who you were created to be, and his love is enough. Alissa, you are enough! You are not the lie, so stop believing it!"

Today, I want to ask you the same question concerning all the filters in your life. Who told you that? The Father saw destiny in your dirt and ministry in your mud, even when you created the mess all on your own. Yes, your roots may be exposed, but they can't start growing again unless you first dig and then throw a little dirt on top of them. But let's go a little further than that. Maybe there's no fruit growing in your life (love, joy, peace, etc.) because you're afraid to acknowledge that it needs dirt to thrive.

God created you to live an unfiltered life of relationship with him. So stop filtering yourself! He never asked for perfection. He asked for you to be present. Dirt carries value because it allows your roots to take you deeper than you've ever been before, and it allows the fruit of destiny to grow in your life. When you embrace where you're truly at in your story, that's when you can begin to be perfected in him.

Understand, today, that you determine what grows in your life. You are the soil that determines what lives and what dies. Satan can't kill what he didn't plant, and dirt is nothing more than destiny waiting to happen! Choose to dig so you can let old roots go and new roots grow. Look up toward the Son and push past the dirt with a posture of promise. Because, friend, you're fixing to show everybody watching you that it's possible to bloom amidst the impossible.

You are the soil that determines what lives and

what dies!

Confession

I'm tired of feeling like I have to cover up the dirt in my life ...
Instead, I'm learning to embrace it.

Truth

He saw destiny in your dirt before it ever had the chance to become
clean.

Journal entry
July 5, 2017

Hello,

I'm home. I arrived last night … and the reality of change in my life
is so present it's almost haunting.

When I pulled up to my house after being gone for so long, the grass
was tall, and the water in the kiddie pool was green. My trash outside
stank from not being taken to the curb during my three-week absence,
and my driveway led to an empty space, reminding me of where my
husband's truck used to sit. I got out of the car thinking, *I've got so much
to do … by myself … without a spouse. I don't know that I can do this
alone. Are we really getting divorced? Is this real?*

I stepped up to the house with my suitcase dragging behind me, and
as I flung open the door, the smell of emptiness filled my nostrils. Our
home is an older home. So when it hasn't been lived in for several weeks,
it develops the smell of vacancy. You can imagine the reality of my life
slapping me in the face with the literal stench of loneliness, old

memories, and lack of presence. Vacancy seems to have marked my life in too many ways to count.

I slid to the floor as the door latched behind me, and tears filled my eyes. "God! I'm mad as hell!" I yelled. "Who gave him the right to uproot our family and destroy our stability? Who said he could push the dynamics of a completely different mother-daughter relationship onto me? How come I'm the one who has to pick up the pieces for the kids when I'm in pieces myself? How come I have to be the one to file for divorce when this was his choice? Where are YOU, God?! Why aren't you fixing this? Why has my husband left us?"

And something happened in that moment. Something snapped deep down inside me while I was sitting on my kitchen floor against the door. Rage suddenly filled my heart. Pain filled my emotions. Confusion filled my mind. And I found myself tearing through the house screaming with anger, crying uncontrollably, and throwing every single memory I had of my husband into boxes in the guest room. I cussed. I yelled at God. I broke pictures. I tore up letters.

I lost my mind.

But in some strange way, I felt the mind of Christ begin to speak at the same time.

It's okay to feel. It's okay to hurt. It's okay to scream, cry, break stuff, and maybe even cuss a little. Lord knows I did all of that today. I had a moment of release. All the emotions I'd bottled up came pouring out at once. But what I'm finding to be true is that, even during an epic meltdown, feelings aren't fact; they are fickle. And I'm learning to trust

God with the fractured pieces of my heart so that faith can remain my constant.

Three days ago, I filed for divorce. I never thought I'd do that. I never thought I'd be the one paying a woman a large sum of money to erase nearly ten years of marriage for me—and to erase the vow I'd made to a man I loved dearly. Yet here I am.

I was told that the papers will be ready to review and sign within the next several weeks if agreed upon.

Is this real?

My marriage is over. Yet somehow, even amidst the rage ... I am okay. I have peace. I have faith. And as crazy as it seems, some kind of healing happened today in the loudness of my anger. "Why, God?! Why weren't you faithful? Why did you fail my family? Why didn't you restore this? I want an answer!"

And then I heard the Father's voice whisper, Because there's only one thing I can never do. I can never go against someone's will. I am not punishing you. I am positioning you for more.

Those words marked me forever. They instantly changed the atmosphere I was in and left me at peace. That moment will forever be engraved on my heart.

So here I sit, on my back porch, writing this entry. My face is red and swollen from crying too many tears to count, and I have no idea where my husband is or who he's with at this moment. Still, I can't help but think, *I wonder if he even cares that we've arrived home?*

But here's the truth …

We *haven't* arrived home. We're a different family than we were when we left.

We are stronger.

We are wiser.

We are more aware.

The truth is, we left broken, but I've determined that we came back brave.

I see the future as a mystery, but there's hope there. There's peace there. There's love there. There's joy there. There are dreams there.

Yes, I may smell the stench of vacancy at the moment, but the aroma of victory will surround my story when God is done with me.

My heart hurts, but I can't help but be reminded of the promise of God on my life and my kids' lives.

He will prove his faithfulness.

I will remain confident that I will see the goodness of the Lord!

Alissa

Chapter 4: *Trust*

I'm not sure when it happened exactly. Perhaps it's from being raised in ministry all my life and getting to see, behind the scenes, just how mean church people can really be. Perhaps it was the moment my best friend decided to take her own life, and I realized, for the first time, that I can't save people from themselves. Or maybe it was the moment I was date-raped at fourteen years old by the first boy to ever say he loved me. Regardless, trust—with a reputation that always seemed to disappoint—left a bad taste in my mouth somewhere along the way.

Let's face it, people are tough to figure out, and trust is hard to give away. Personally, I had become a professional at holding people at arm's-length and questioning their ability to be *for me* rather than against. That five-letter word, trust, had left me wounded, scarred, and stamped with regret too many times throughout my life; because of that, the struggle had become **REAL**.

I've heard it quoted all my life, and I'm sure you have as well:

Trust in the Lord with all your heart and lean not on your own

understanding;

In all your ways acknowledge him, and he shall direct your paths.

(Proverbs 3:5-6, NKJV)

I knew that scripture to be a cute verse pastors would throw in the face of hurting people, whose situations they couldn't understand or give explanation to. It was used, with a pat on the back, to bring comfort and peace of mind to people as their pastor said, "My dear brother/sister, God is working it out, even when you may not understand how. You just need to trust him."

The problem I have with that is, in all my years of being raised as a pastor's kid—and being in full-time ministry as an adult—I've never once heard anyone take the stage and address a particular issue: What happens when the one you're having a hard time trusting isn't people, or even yourself? What if the one you can't trust is God?

For the first time in my life, that question was colliding with my faith. I knew in my heart that I had to confront it before I could take a step forward, and that made me angry. I became angry at God, angry at my myself, angry at my ex-husband, angry at the church, and angry at my pastors. No one could answer that question for me, and the longer I went without a solution, the angrier I became.

Trust was a difficult task, in and of itself, but trusting God was proving to be even more difficult during that season of my life. My marriage was falling apart, my then-husband was MIA most of the time, and I'd been left with no answers from him. And my girls were broken-hearted, with questions of their own.

You're asking me to trust God? Then tell me how! You want me to trust him with my whole heart? What heart? My heart was shattered into a million memories, all over what I used to call "life," and now I'm left with a pile of rubble.

Confession #4: Trust didn't seem logical, because God didn't seem

reliable!

Have you ever been there before? Have you ever found yourself smack-dab in the middle of a situation that was undeniably unexplainable? Have you ever found yourself pacing the floor, begging God to help you understand something ... anything ... the smallest thing, just so you could make some kind of sense out of it?

Maybe it wasn't divorce for you. Maybe it was the loss of a loved one you were standing with, in faith, for healing. Maybe it was a miscarriage after believing God for a child for so long. Maybe it was rape or molestation, and not understanding how a "good God" could allow something so horrible to be done to you. Maybe it was the fact that you jumped off a ledge, in faith, because God asked you to, but now it seems like one thing after another is falling apart.

Whatever your story is, I want you to know I was there. I was in that place of unexplained pain, and I found myself angry; I found myself confused; I found myself tired, hurting, and most of all … I was mad as hell. Questions began to fill my mind, but one, in particular, burned the hottest: *God, how can I trust you when you're letting my marriage fall apart?*

I've learned in life to only ask God a question if I'm ready for the answer. And I remember exactly where I was. I remember exactly what I was wearing. I remember the exact day, time, and moment that I got my answer. It will forever be etched on my heart because it was the first day I began to trust God with its pieces.

I had just gotten home from being in Kansas for three long weeks. I went because I needed some time to unplug from the chaos, get away from the surroundings of pain, and spend some time seeking direction concerning my marriage and that ugly word "divorce."

When I got back into town, I took my kids to my parents' house so I could do some unpacking without them around. I remember foolishly building hope in my heart, thinking that maybe—just maybe—my husband would be home when I arrived. Maybe God was going to turn it around. Maybe my husband would be waiting for me so we could work everything out, and I could call my lawyer to withdraw the divorce papers.

But as I pulled around the corner of my street, I remember feeling my heart break apart in pain—his truck was still missing from its spot in our driveway.

I needed a breather.

I needed some space.

I needed to scream.

I needed to throw something.

I needed a release from the rage.

I needed answers!

When I walked into my home, my emotions shot from low to high so fast that I found myself on a roller coaster ride right there in the middle of the house. I went from deep sorrow and crying to immediate anger and rage in just about five minutes flat. I'm not sure what snapped inside me after that, but I found myself wiping the tears from my eyes, peeling myself off the kitchen floor, and furiously storming toward the guest room with empty boxes in hand.

You have to understand something here, divorce was not an option for me. It wasn't my choice, and even though I'm the one who filed the papers, I'm not the one who gave up—he's the one who made the decision to quit on our family. I loved my husband, and when I said my vows, I full-heartedly meant, "till death do us part." I'd done everything in my power to save our marriage during that time, and despite our journey, I'd spiritually stood in the gap for my husband for years. Twelve years of being with him, nearly ten years of marriage, and two baby girls being born into the world was too much of an investment for me to willingly throw away. So I decided, a long time ago, to fight for him until

God told me otherwise. Restoration was the promise I'd stood on for two solid months during our separation, and I was angry at God for not allowing it to take place.

How is this possible? How can God allow a marriage to fall apart when marriage was God's idea in the first place? How can his plan for my life be a broken family for my daughters? How come he used my ministry to see restoration in countless other peoples' marriages but is willing to let mine fall apart? Isn't he a good God? Isn't he able? Isn't his Word true?

During that season, I was quick to obey and willing to submit to each and every thing I felt the Holy Spirit ask me to do. No matter how unreasonable, unfair, or crazy it seemed, I trusted that God was going to restore my marriage. So I listened and dug deep inside my heart, pulling out every ounce of strength I had, to trust him as I obeyed. But it didn't seem like my obedience was honored or seen, because my marriage still ended in divorce.

Why God?! How come I did everything you asked me to do and you still didn't come through? How come my obedience didn't mean a thing to you?

Did God remember those late nights where my husband never came home to me and the kids? Did he remember asking me to anoint my husband's pillow with oil and lay over it, interceding for him as he was out all night? Did he remember me crying out to him for my husband's life, calling, and purpose as my heart was breaking at the same time? Did he remember telling me to greet my husband with a kiss and an "I love you," no matter how late he came home, how bad he smelled, or how guilty he looked? Did he remember telling me to protect the kids in love and grace by celebrating their father, no matter how many days he went without talking to them or seeing them? Did he remember asking me to pray for the woman he had shown me in a detailed dream, while telling me that my husband was giving his heart to someone else? Did he remember the letters of love, forgiveness, and affirmation he had led me to write to my husband when I was broken, rejected, and abandoned? Did he remember the nights where my kids cried themselves to sleep and he had me sing songs of worship over them, even amid my own pain?

Do you remember, God? Because I did all of that! I did that and everything else you asked of me! Why didn't you do your part? Why didn't you restore this brokenness? Why did you go back on your promise?

Trust was broken in my life, restoration seemed to be a lie, and obedience had let me down. Have you been there before? Have you felt that? Have you struggled with the idea that trust doesn't seem logical because God doesn't seem reliable? Because I've felt the anger. I've processed the confusion, and the whirlwind of emotions, of what exactly I was supposed to believe when it came to my feelings and my faith.

And let me tell you, there was a war raging inside me over which belief was going to win, but I still remember the evening I began to trust God with the pieces. I remember the moment that all the rage began to release, and rest began to find a place in me for the first time in a long time. I'd collapsed in the guest room floor with boxes of my husband's things all around me. He had told the kids and I, right before we took our trip to Kansas, that he'd gotten a new house and was moving out of ours. As I sat there with broken memories all around, I found that the quiet whisper of the Father's love was louder than my rage in that moment.

I had one aching question, "God, why weren't you faithful to restore?"

He had one quiet response, Because there's only one thing I can never do. I can never go against someone's will. I am not punishing you. I am positioning you for more.

I am not punishing you. I am positioning you for

more.

I don't know where you're struggling in your life when it comes to trusting God. I know it doesn't make any sense, and you're doing all you can to just keep going, but let me reach through these pages and grab you by the hand when I say this.

Friend, God isn't punishing you. He's positioning you for more. Just trust him.

Nothing made sense to me at that time of my life, but looking back on it now, I see a detailed plan of purpose that beautifully began to unfold, all because I learned how to trust God with the pieces of my life. I had to learn that no matter how much pain was written on the fabric of my story, he saw every bit of it and still promised me a future full of hope and good things! He knew my husband's answer would be no. He knew my husband would choose to walk away for another woman. He knew the cost would be great and our intended future would look different. And despite it all, God also knew that he is faithful to always show us his love, no matter how hard we fight his plan, purpose, and will for our life. His grace will always show its face and give us one more chance to say yes. My obedience was a picture of God's love for my husband, but without me even knowing it, it was also a picture of promise. God was positioning me for more and preparing me for the next steps of my process toward restoration.

Let's look at this again:

> Trust in the Lord with all your heart and lean not on your
> own understanding;
> In all your ways acknowledge him, and he shall direct your
> path. (Proverbs 3:5-6, NKJV)

I'd never studied this scripture much before, but what I found during that time of my life was that the word *lean* means to rest, rely on, or derive support from. Let me ask you today, How can you lean on something that you don't quite understand? How can you rest when nothing makes sense? How can you rely on something that seems broken? How can you draw support from something that seems to be working against you?

Can I tell you that sometimes you have to find peace within the answers you'll never receive? It's not your job to understand it all. It's your job to lean on the one who directs your feet and places you on the path of promise.

Listen, if you don't truly know Jesus for yourself, then you will always question his ability to hold your heart. Maybe this is a place for you to become more aware of who he is so he can put you back together again.

Our natural response as humans is to give *ourselves* the job of gatekeeper over our heart—and we do it well. We faithfully stand guard, protecting our hearts, and build walls around the areas that are hurting us. Our intention is to prevent further injury from taking place, but without realizing it, we end up hurting ourselves instead of finding a safe space for healing. Even though our effort was meant to keep others out of the vulnerable places, we find that we're actually trapping ourselves inside of those wounds. In doing so, we end up holding ourselves captive to painful places and memories that we never had to be bound to in the first place.

But hear me, friend. How can the Father truly bring healing, guidance, and love to a heart when it's separated by filters and walls? How can you truly receive the acceptance you need when you're not allowing him access? How can you truly receive healing when you're hindering him from touching the hurt areas?

Filters and walls destroy our lives worse than the wounds we're trying to mend. You can't truly trust someone if you don't ever allow them the opportunity to prove that they're trustworthy.

Ask yourself this today, Have I been standing as gatekeeper for so long that I've forgotten who the keeper of my heart truly is?

Let me share with you a story that helped me understand the importance of trusting God with my whole heart. It was my first year of Bible college, and, like many other college students, I spent most of my free time at the mall. Of course, I was doing nothing more than window shopping because the only money I had was spent on ramen noodles, toilet paper, and laundry soap.

Nevertheless, while dreaming about all the clothes I would buy when I became rich and famous, I decided to take my diamond wedding ring to the jewelry store to be cleaned (for free, duh). When I arrived to pick it up, they proceeded to tell me that I had ten small diamonds loose and desperately needing repaired. I was devastated! For me, repair money meant rent money, and at that moment, I only had ramen money. So the odds of me getting my ring fixed were slim to none.

But that ring was a one-of-a-kind design, specially made through a jeweler in Kansas, so I decided to go talk to the designer himself. With a weekend trip and a visit to the jeweler planned, I was anxious to see what could be done before I took the word of the other jeweler and broke the bank. But what he found after much inspection, polishing, and even more inspecting, shocked me. He looked me in the face and said he'd come to the conclusion that my ring didn't need any repairs at all. In fact, after a much-needed cleaning job, it looked just as good as new! His words were, "This ring was made with precision and close detail. Those diamonds aren't going anywhere. The other jeweler just wanted to give you a bill that says it's broke so they can make bank."

Y'all, how many times do we allow people the opportunity to inspect our hearts and then stamp us with a mark labeled "fragile" when the truth is that we're far from it?

Trusting the process toward your promise means trusting the truth behind your value. In the same way that people look for the mark of dirt on your life, they'll also look for the damage in your life. If you aren't careful, people will speak lies about your condition, declaring that you're broken and in pieces. Their words will leave you with a distorted view of who you are and could keep you in a mentality of needing repaired, when the reality is that you're being repositioned.

Trusting the process toward your promise means trusting the truth behind your value.

Friend, the truth about your heart is that the sacrifice has already been made! You're not broken at all! In fact, you've been made *whole* in Christ! He marked you with destiny and purpose from the beginning of time, and he sealed it with a promise by saying, "It is finished," when he hung on that cross. Stop taking your heart into your own hands, and—for the love of coffee—stop taking it to people who have no business inspecting it in the first place! If anyone has any right to be trusted, it's the designer and creator himself! Start trusting the one who formed you in his hands and gave you the beat you feel inside your chest! I think you'll be shocked to find that you aren't broken at all. You're simply being repositioned for more.

Confession

Trust didn't seem logical, because God didn't seem reliable!

Truth

God isn't punishing you. He's positioning you.

Journal entry
July 10, 2017

Glass House,

She's like a glass house who's frame of certainty is still standing strong amid shattered pieces, all because she knew she could be rebuilt.

She stands in the knowing that she may be shattered, but now that also means she's sharp. Now she can take those edges that once hurt and cut out the places that no longer fit. The places that hindered. The places that drug her down. Now she can carve out a new identity for herself; an identity that matches the woman she always knew she could be.

What do you do when your reflection—the person you knew yourself to be—is shattered in pieces all around you? The answer is this, you simply allow your frame to stand tall, even in transparency, because it's in that place that your faith finds the freedom to be rebuilt!

When you're shook to your core and feel as though you might crumble once more ... you stand! Even when you find yourself staring at the shattered reflection of what once was … you stand! Even when the edges cut deep, and the pain is real … you stand! You allow the pain to carve out identity, and you don't waver. You don't sway. You don't doubt who you're being built to become. You don't allow your *present* to dictate your *promise*!

You simply stand.

It's in that place—the place of brokenness and shattered identity—that the identity-maker will come in and mark you with the loving touch of a father.

He will rebuild you.

He will put the pieces back together differently.

He will create a new heart within the mess.

He will gently sort through the wreckage and begin to speak purpose over the pieces.

It's on the frame of faith that he'll begin to rebuild identity and purpose once more. That's where he'll allow you to be put on display—not to be mean, but to allow others to see what it looks like to be rebuilt and how to allow God to create beauty in the midst of chaos.

Alissa

Chapter 5: *Build*

Maybe it's not always about trying to fix something broken. Maybe
it's about starting over and creating something better.

—Unknown

**That quote was one of many I printed out and taped onto my
mirror during that season of my life.** I found it by scrolling
through Pinterest the day after having a meltdown. It was the middle of
summertime, and I'd been invited to attend a pool party at my friend's
home. Eager to get my mind off all the pain I'd been carrying around
every second of every day, I decided it would be good for me to get out
of the house with the girls and go

have some fun. But as I was driving over to her home, I realized this would be my first gathering without my husband.

What will I say? Should I act like nothing is going on? Do I answer people when they ask where he is? Will all our friends get suspicious? Am I ready to address this right now? Do I need to be sure to shelter the girls from hearing these questions?

Once we pulled up to the house, the girls shot out of the car with excitement. With their hair bouncing freely and their little feet dancing with joy, they ran right up to the door and let themselves inside. I, on the other hand, couldn't seem to find the willpower or strength to move. I sat in the driveway panicking as the questions in my mind flooded my head with anxiety. The minutes drug on, and before I knew it, my phone began to light up with text messages from my friends.

Are you coming inside?

Are you ok?

The girls are in the pool now, so I was just checking on you.

And just when I thought I'd finally caught my breath and could pull myself out of the car, my eyes caught a glimpse of my hand on the steering wheel ... and it stopped me dead in my tracks.

In but a second, I realized that nearly nine years earlier I'd been reminded of a lesson taught by a ring that sat on my hand every single day. The lesson was about the importance of trusting the designer's word that you're whole, over the word of others that says you're broken, and it's something I—quite literally—carried around daily. ... This time was different for me because that reminder was absent, and I was left with the imprint of a broken reality staring me in the face.

What do you do when a broken promise has imprinted on your life? What do you do when you feel like life has marked you with rejection, abandonment, pain, disappointment, failure, and hopelessness? I've heard many stories that revolve around the dirt found within broken promises. And no matter how different our backgrounds, beliefs, or stories may be, I've found that the pain behind them proves to be one of the hardest things to move forward from.

Tia's story was much like mine. Her broken promise stemmed from a marriage that began with vows and ended with abandonment. She reached out to me with a Facebook message:

> Hi Alissa, my name is Tia. I found you when you and your husband were doing worship live on Facebook. Today my husband decided that he no longer wants to be with me and my kids. He's leaving for a new life in Kentucky, and I'm completely beside myself. He's made so many promises, and now he's just leaving us.
>
> I know you know how this part feels. Any advice for me getting through the next few months of divorce, moving, and becoming a single mom after seventeen years of marriage? I need help and don't have anywhere to turn!"

Julie was different than Tia and me. She may not have said the vows of "I do," but she had the promise of "happily ever after," and it ended before it ever began. Her story read:

You don't' know me, but I need your help. My fiancé and I have been together for three years, and I just recently found out that he's been talking to an exotic dancer for the past two months. We got engaged last year, and I found out last night that he's been with her every night, when he was supposed to be at work. He promised me that he was bettering himself and working toward our future together.

He's broken so many promises and I don't know what to do. She shows her body to men nonstop, but I'm committed to only him. Why did he just throw us away? This is the second time I've been left for someone else, and I'm tired of not being enough. Why doesn't anyone want me? Why did he ask me to marry him, and then decide to leave me? This hurts so bad, and I don't know who to talk to because I'm embarrassed and don't know why this is happening.

Eric's story was one of tragedy, and how promise can be ripped from your heart without warning or fault. He wrote:

> I don't know who else to turn to, but I heard your story on social media and wanted to reach out. I recently got engaged to the woman of my dreams. She was everything I prayed for and more. After a heartbreaking divorce, I never thought I'd find anyone else to love. I held on to the promise that God was working all things out for good, but last week I got a call around 10 p.m. that changed my life.
>
> My fiancé was in a head-on collision and passed away on the scene.
>
> Why is this happening? How do I move forward from here? I don't quite know what I'm supposed to do, but I don't feel like I can go to the church for help. Why do bad things happen to good people? Do you have any advice?

Jessica and Tim held tightly to the promise of their children living a life full of joy, purpose, and love, while it all seemed to be falling apart. They wrote me this:

> Alissa, we've followed your ministry for quite some time.

We found you on Periscope years ago and have been watching your journey unfold. We wanted to message you in hopes that you would have some advice for us. Our son, Jeremy, is fifteen years old and is extremely rebellious, distant, and has even made comments about suicide. Our hearts break for him, and we don't know what we are to do about it.

We've taken him to several churches to seek help, gotten him counseling, put him on meds for his anxiety, and prayed relentlessly for him. It's putting a major strain on our marriage and family.

My husband drinks, and I'm left feeling like cigarettes are my favorite place to turn. Why can't anyone seem to help us? Why does the Word promise that if you train up a child in the way they should go, they won't depart from it ... yet here we are? We are ashamed and don't know who to talk to.

As I sit here in my office surrounded by pages from my journals, index cards filled with notes, and pictures to remind me of my "why" behind the purpose of this book, I've received a great reminder from Halley. My Facebook inbox showed me her message of broken promises, and how they can imprint your life in ways that keep you from moving forward with happiness. Some of her message reads:

Hi Alissa! I'm really having a difficult time right now and need some guidance. My mom and dad divorced shortly after I was born. I was raised by my grandparents, who gained custody of me at three years old, due to my parents' neglect and drug use.

I had a great life and was raised in church, but I always yearned for a close relationship with my mom. I see my mom now, but she's still full of broken promises. Every time I think, "This is going to be the time that she actually loves me and does what she says she will," she just disappoints me again. This has affected me so much in every aspect of my life, but really, I see it when it comes to my romantic relationships.

I push people away with my constant thoughts that they're going to leave me or break my heart. I feel unworthy of love, and like I'm just not a person that anyone cares to be around. Do you have any advice for me to get over this hurt from my childhood? Because it's ruining my life!

I never quite understood why there are so many broken people who don't trust the church with the pieces of their heart, until I became more broken than I'd ever been. If there was ever a flaw that I saw the most within the walls of religion, it would be the lack of ability to handle fragile hearts with care. We've failed in providing a safe place for people to be rebuilt, and I believe that's because we don't quite understand how to handle brokenness ourselves. What do we do? How do we fix it?

What I've seen is the sad reality that our auditoriums fill up with people who are secretly hiding pieces that never could quite fit within the mold of religion, so they just don't talk about them. They walk around, filtered with plastic masks of joy and fake freedom, while they carry the weight of empty spaces they don't know how to fill and lonely pieces they don't know where to keep hidden. And that doesn't even include those who refuse to hide their brokenness at church and choose loneliness in the space of their own home and world.

And the biggest problem we have is that *we don't talk about it.*

Confession #5 : For most of my life, brokenness kept me bound to

silence.

As a pastor's kid who was raised in church and marked by religion, I learned early on how to shove the broken pieces of my life (and all the question marks) underneath the rug. But that wasn't something my parents taught me to do. My family was incredibly open and unashamed to talk about our issues freely in the safe space of our home. The cover-up behavior was learned within the church walls; it was almost like an unspoken rule that everyone understood, but no one talked about.

With hands lifted, a smile smeared from one corner of my mouth to the other, and cute little handshakes (paired with a pat on the back), you'd never know that this pastor's daughter, along with many others, was more broken than she was whole.

As I take the time to sit with people and listen to their unfiltered stories, I become more confident in the reality that us humans have more answers to offer than we have questions to ask. The problem, though, is that we've been taught to sit in silence. We've been trained to understand that dirt makes us dirty and filth should be covered up. And without even recognizing that learned behavior, we choose to navigate our brokenness in silence and suffer alone.

If only we could learn to let the filters down and share our stories without the fear of being judged. Only then could we see the freedom it would bring to our lives and to countless others who feel they have no one to talk to.

It's during those times that some of us are lucky enough to find the grace of a loving God, while others aren't so lucky at all. I've seen many come out of life's tragedies closer to their destiny than they've ever been. But there are others (like my best friend), who end up taking their own life out of desperation to find some relief from the pain. No matter where you fall on the spectrum of life, one thing is the same for us all: Brokenness leaves you feeling hopelessly and utterly alone, and it leads you to believe that no one could possibly understand what it is you're going through.

Y'all, let me stop right here and scream the truth about brokenness from these pages, because the truth is …

You are NOT alone!

There are more people, like Tia and Eric, who understand exactly where you are. And still others, like Janet and Tim, who need to hear your story just as badly as you need to hear theirs.

The truth is, brokenness is a bondage meant to keep you silent. But you were not created for silence, my friend! You were created with the ability to build a backbone with the broken pieces, and that backbone has a voice that needs to be heard! You could be the answer to someone else owning their truth!

The truth is, brokenness is a bondage meant to keep you silent.

If only we could all learn to unfilter the reality of our lives and live free from shame and guilt by sharing our story, then we'd begin to see so much more healing take place, and the world wouldn't be so lonely after all.

Take it from Halley, if it weren't for me sharing some of my story with her today, she might not have found purpose in her ability to move forward from her pain. What would have happened if I allowed myself to believe the lie of brokenness and remained bound to silence? I dare to say it would have disabled me from building with the pieces of my life once more and kept me from helping people like Julie find their value in the hope of Jesus instead of in the promise of a man's last name. If brokenness had ruled my life when writing this book, sharing my truth behind all the things that said I was dirty might not be my reality. And the scary part is that silence could have stopped me from coming face to face with the promise of my destiny.

Here's the thing. Your destiny is found within the dirt you're sitting in right now. It's found within the pieces in front of you that you're seeing as stumbling blocks. It's found within the pain you're navigating through at this moment. No matter what it looks like. No matter who did it and how it came about. This right here is your moment to build with the broken pieces of your life. This is the moment for you to decide that broken promises might have imprinted you, but *destiny* has marked you forever. So what will you do with it? What will you believe? The only thing greater than the tragedy you had to go through is what you don't do with it. You possess the power to allow this to break you or to build you.

I wish I could tell you that divorce was the only broken area of my life that damaged me as badly as it did, but the truth is that it wasn't. I wish I could tell you that tragedy wasn't a familiar place for me to navigate alone, but that wouldn't be true either. The only difference is that, this time, I chose not to sit within filtered silence and suffer by myself.

This time, I chose to walk unfiltered and talk about the broken areas of my life in order to build once more.

This time, I decided to allow God to put the pieces back together differently so I could (excuse my language) be the badass woman I was created to be.

This time, I chose to see the broken edges as a tool sharp enough to cut away all the things in my life that were holding me back from who it is I truly am.

I chose to recognize the pieces as *purpose,* and I decided to stop allowing my pain to steal my voice.

Throughout the process, I found other areas of my heart that had been neglected, infected, damaged, and forgotten about. I started a journey that would ultimately lead to my destiny. It's a journey that I'll continue to walk down until the day I die. It requires me to dig deep, sort through the pieces, release filters that fit me like a glove, and own the truth for myself.

The words I found myself pinning to my Pinterest board couldn't have been more life-giving for me:

Maybe it's not always about trying to fix something broken. Maybe it's about starting over and creating something better.

—Unknown

If I could tell you anything, friend, it would be this ... life isn't over for you; it's simply falling into order. Sometimes you must change your perspective in order to embrace your process.

Life isn't over for you; it's simply falling into order. Sometimes you must change your perspective in order to embrace your process.

And maybe you don't know where to go from here. Maybe you feel like you don't have the strength to move forward from the place you're at right now. But wherever it is, I want to meet you where you are by saying this is where it all began for me. It's where I began to pick myself up off the ground to reclaim my destiny and own the truth of who I am. It's how I found promise in the pieces and allowed myself to find the strength I needed to rebuild.

You can do this. If there's one thing I have zero doubt about, it's your ability to own your future and see promise fulfilled in your life! The question that remains is, are you ready?

If so, I can promise you that you're not alone. The lie will come to tell you that you are. It'll come to say that no one understands you, and that this journey is meant to be a lonely road. But remember, that is a lie! If you have no one else in your life who's willing to take your hand during this season, then please know I'm right here with you. I am confident that you were made for this moment, and with God by your side, **YOU CANNOT FAIL!**

> He heals the brokenhearted
>
> and binds up their wounds. (Psalm 147:3, NKJV)

Confession

For most of my life, brokenness kept me bound to silence.

Truth

You were created with the ability to build a backbone with the broken pieces, and that backbone has a voice that needs to be heard!

Journal entry

May 5, 2016

Hello, (One year prior)

My pages are no stranger to being filled with dreams given to me in the night hour. Since the age of eight, I've marked off one dream after another in my journals as I watch them come to pass. If there's anything I've experienced to be more real, it would be the voice of God while I sleep. Over the years, I've learned to separate that voice from what my momma would call "crazy pizza dreams." And last night definitely wasn't a pizza dream. I woke up shook to my core and felt like the voice of God was speaking to me vividly.

Most of the time, when I wake up from a dream that I feel, down in my gut, was from God, I'm pretty aware of the meaning behind it. But this dream has been interesting for me because it doesn't make much sense at the moment.

When I woke up this morning, I felt my heart beating out of my chest. I was sweating, breathing hard, and I could remember everything in vivid detail. I knew this dream didn't match up to my life at this current moment, but I feel like it's a warning for what's to come. And of course, I record all my dreams, so here it is.

If you can imagine Snow White mixed with Pleasantville, in real time, that would be a picture of what this looked like. Everywhere I looked, there was no color in sight; it was a black-and-white canvas. And I found myself all alone.

I was running through a forest of trees that became giants, with hands pulling on me from every side while I tried to get away. It remined me of Snow White running through the woods, right before she found the small cottage where the seven dwarfs lived. All I felt was terror as I ran frantically, looking for a place where I could find safety. When I spotted a building in the distance, the air was cold and my heart was beating as fast as it could. As I approached it, with a fling of the door, and ran inside, I started to pray that this nightmare would end.

Then to my surprise, I found that although none of this made sense, the inside of this building was familiar territory. In fact, it was my parents' church. I began running through the halls, opening doors, and calling out for my husband and family ... but no one would respond. There was nothing but silence, cold air, and black-and-white surroundings showing no sign of life.

As I sat on one of the chairs in the auditorium, I heard the thing that was chasing me down begin to approach the building. A noise like intense wind started to sweep through the halls and, without warning, everything in sight began to be sucked up and pulled out of the building, one by one.

I hid behind one of the wooden doors, screaming as I watched it all disappear before my eyes. I was filled with fear and uncertainty and didn't know what exactly was going on, or what would happen next.

Where is my family? Why is this happening? When will it stop?

Once everything had disappeared, the wind became silent. I found myself all alone. Trembling with fear, I sat there, not knowing what to do next.

Then a voice began to speak to me, "Alissa, come outside."

"NO!" I screamed out. "Why would I do that? What if that *thing* is waiting for me?"

I heard the voice once more, "Trust me. It doesn't make sense right now, but I need you to take a step out of the door."

When I pulled myself from behind that wooden door, trying desperately to keep my knees from shaking, the light between the crack of the doorway caught my eye. I carefully pushed the door open as pops of color filled the air. I stepped out from a world of black and white, and into a world of color, as my foot crossed the threshold of the empty building that used to be familiar and entered a new world I didn't recognize.

I walked down the streets filled with wonder, admiring the houses and their grand designs. But one house, in particular, caught my attention when I saw my parents walk inside carrying food. The driveway was lined with stunning, vintage cars, and the windows were as big as doors, with expensive curtains pulled to the side. I stepped into the yard to catch a glimpse of who was inside and what everyone was doing, and I couldn't believe my eyes.

The people inside were my family, and the woman welcoming them in was *me*!

I saw a dining room table, set for dinner, as my sisters and parents took their seats. Of course, the first thoughts that came to my mind were, *Where are my kids? Is my husband here with us?* And not long after, I saw my girls run around the corner and a man come and kiss me on my cheek. Startled, I remember saying out loud, "That's not my husband! Who is that, and what is this place?"

That's when I heard the voice speak something profound before I woke up, "Sometimes I have to swallow up and get rid of the life you knew in order to give you the life I always intended for you to have."

I woke up confused but shook. I'm not sure what all of this means, but one thing is for certain ... something is stirring in my spirit, and I need to be prepared for what comes next.

Alissa

Chapter 6: *Pieces*

bro ·ken[1]

ˈbrō kən

adjective

1. Dead inside. Torn apart. You lost everything.

Have you ever been so emotionally broken that you could feel it throughout your entire body?

I did a study on emotional pain and wasn't surprised to find that research has shown that our brains react to heartbreak in the same way they react to physical pain. In 2011, *Medical News Today* analyzed forty people in New York City who felt immense rejection in one way or another. During the study, they were asked to look at photos of friends, family, and exes (whom they directed their pain and rejection toward) while their brains were scanned for changes in activity. In comparison, the same forty people underwent scans to recognize changes in activity as they underwent pain on their forearms similar to a hot cup of coffee being poured on them.

As the study was evaluated, the research proved that several of the same areas of the brain became active when the body felt either emotional or physical pain. The research went on to say it appears that rejection is in a class of its own emotionally and is similar to physical pain, with the ability to affect people in a tangible way[2]. (We'll be covering feelings and the emotional process toward promise later in part 1.)

Recognizing where you're at emotionally, mentally, and spiritually is step number one when it comes to moving forward and being able to build toward your promise of destiny. It may seem like common sense for some, but for many of us, we want progress without the process. But guys, that doesn't work. I truly believe we avoid the responsibility to recognize where we're at because we think we're protecting our hearts from further damage and pain. It may be innocent, but if we aren't careful, we'll bypass areas—to save ourselves from sorting through the wreckage—that desperately need to be addressed.

One of the biggest questions I had when I realized my husband wasn't coming home to us was, "God, why didn't you restore it?"

His answer was simple, Because there's only one thing I can't do, and that's to go against someone's will.

I've said it before, and I'll say it again because it's worth repeating: Jesus can't touch what you don't allow him to.

You are the answer to the restoration in your life. And part of owning your truth is being able to take responsibility when it comes to the pieces of your heart. We skip this part so many times because we think it means we're taking full responsibility for how the brokenness came about. That is not true! It doesn't mean you're the one responsible for the circumstances; it means you're taking full responsibility for being rebuilt, whether it was you who did the breaking or not.

It wasn't until I allowed myself to see the reality of where I truly was (mentally, emotionally, and spiritually) that I began to ask myself questions I never felt I had the freedom to ask before.

What is it that I'm truly afraid of?

What, specifically, has hurt me?

What voice have I been listening to, for years, that's kept me from healing and becoming the person I know I can be?

What unaddressed wounds in my past have allowed new ones to emerge now?

What do I want in life?

Who am I, and who do I want to be?

What part did I play (if any) in allowing all of this to come about?

Do I want to keep life how it is right now, or do I want to create a new one?

I sat down one morning at 4 a.m., with a paper and pen, to assess the damage in my life. It's not easy to unfilter the person you've been known as—the person you've allowed yourself to hide behind for so long.

Because as my daddy used to say, "If you tell a lie long enough, you'll begin to believe it's true." But I knew taking responsibility for the pieces of my life had to be the first step I took in walking toward my destiny, and, friend, it has to be yours too. Because listen, you can never assess the damage in your life unless you're willing to address the lies you've been believing about yourself.

You can never assess the damage in your life unless you're willing to address the lies you've been believing about yourself.

Confession #6: I used to wear my brokenness as a badge.

For so many years, I carried the weight of pain and hurt on my shoulders—from things as major as rape to those as small as the mean girl in my life who said I'd never be pretty enough. No matter where it came from, I allowed myself to believe the lie of brokenness, and I let it tell me who I was in the silence of my hurt. It would scream that my rapist was the source of my trust issues because he stole my purity at age fourteen. It said the porn addiction of the men who hurt my heart was the source of my low self-esteem and eating disorders. It whispered to me that the voices of the family members who laughed at my dreams were the reasons why I'd never achieve any at all. It said the church-hurt I experienced, under the microscope of being a pastor's kid, was the reason for my rebellion and party days.

All those lies, and so many more, screamed out my name as I sat in silence because I never felt like I could truly talk about them. They labeled me with badges that bound me to false truths about who I was and kept me from taking responsibility for my own life. And the longer I wore those badges, the more I began to believe the voice that yelled, "*You* are the reason why you're broken! You deserve every crack and every shattered piece you've received in life. This is who you are, and this is who you'll always be. Just accept it!"

Have you heard any of those lies before? Do you carry your own version of false truths that are keeping you bound to silence?

Listen, friend. The lies will tell you that the things that happened to you have chosen you, and that there's nothing you can do about it. They'll say your anger problems stem from the abuse in your life, and your trust issues will always be there to help protect you and your family from further damage. Or they'll say you're destined to be just like your momma, daddy, grandma, uncle, sister, brother (you name it) just because you share their last name. The voice of false truth will feed you the lie that "this runs in the family," and it'll tell you there's no way around the characteristic issues that you're fighting to overcome. (The list could go on and on, but we'd be here forever if I addressed each falsehood.)

Bottom line, you aren't the only one to buy in to the false truth and swallow it with shame. I was there most of my life, but one day I found the truth to be more real than the lies. What if I told you that you are not what's happened to you, and it has definitely *not* chosen you? What if I told you that your mistake was you choosing to embrace the thing you hate so much and then allowing it to keep you from building again? What if I said you've shackled yourself to the pieces of your life instead of seeing the freedom that lies in creating something new?

Stop allowing yourself to wear badges of brokenness because, if you aren't careful, they'll begin to own who it is that you are.

But listen up. You are *more* than this! You are *more* than the mindset that this is as good as it gets. You are *more* than the voices that try to dictate how you're going to live your life, and how far you're going to get with your dreams. Take the filters down! Assess the damage by addressing the lies that are keeping you from your destiny. The filter of brokenness can no longer be your excuse. You know why? Because I'm here to give you TRUTH.

Are you ready?

The truth is that you are *not* what's happened to you! The truth is that you've been through hell so you can confidently fight like hell to become the person you choose to be. The truth is that there's purpose to be found within the pieces of your life, but you have to make the choice to rebuild.

You set the pace for promise in your life! Whether or not you see it become reality is solely dependent upon you: fact. *You own this life* because *no one else is living it for you*! Will you believe the truth, or will brokenness continue to lie to you about who you are?

I can hear someone thinking right now, Alissa, what if I'm the one who did the breaking in my life and it wasn't someone else's doing?

Well, let me ask you this. When it comes to the wreckage of your life, what if I told you that your biggest role won't be found in the breaking of your own heart? Everyone has moments they're responsible for when it comes to taking ownership of the pieces. And, friend, your biggest role is not found within the breaking; it's found within your ability to own your responsibility to build again. Anyone can break a heart (including their own), but it takes someone with a hell of a story to rebuild with the shattered pieces.

Only a week after I filed for divorce, I was presented with a choice while driving down the highway in Conway, Arkansas. Truth be told, one of the hardest pieces for me to take ownership of was the failure of my marriage. But as I drove through that city, I began to assess the damage. See, it was in that town that he asked me to be his wife. And it was in that town that God was now asking me to trust him with the wreckage.

Can I just say that one of the biggest struggles you'll ever face when it comes to positioning yourself toward promise is learning how to get out of your own way and allow God to work. I learned that lesson while sitting on a two-lane highway in traffic, only two miles from the same, exact spot that the marriage proposal had taken place. And it was there that I was now presented with a new proposal: Am I willing to position myself toward promise once more by building something new?

With bumper-to-bumper traffic backed up for miles, it became evident that a massive wreck had taken place up ahead. I was scanning through the radio as I watched people direct traffic, clean up the mess, take record of the accident, and tend to those who were injured. And as I approached the scene, I began to hear the voice of God gently speak, *Do you see that? That's a picture of the wreckage of your heart. Do you see the traffic behind you? That's a picture of all the answers, provision, success, contacts, opportunity, and promise that's waiting for you. All I need is for you to get out of your own way! I don't need you to collect the pieces off the ground. I need you to trust that I hold them in my hand, and I need you to help me rebuild.*

Hear this. Maybe you feel like you've been shattered into a million pieces of memories right now, and you're desperately trying to collect all of them, one by one, so they don't fall through the cracks of your life. I can say from the bottom of my heart to yours that I know exactly what that feels like. I can tell you firsthand how devastating it is—and how much it sucks—to see life as you know it disappear before your eyes.

I had someone message me today on Instagram, and her words were, "I feel like I've stepped way out of my purpose, and I've let God down.

My heart is heavy, and more than anything, I want this feeling of brokenheartedness to go away."

I want to respond to what you may be feeling right now by sharing with you what I told her.

Listen to me, God is a collector of broken things! He counts the pieces and knows the worth and value behind each tear, each pain, every bit of rejection, and every amount of peace that's been stolen from your life. You HAVE NOT let him down, and he is not angry at you for falling apart! You've simply given him another chance to put you back together the way he intended for you to be built from the beginning.

This is not your undoing! This is simply the beginning of you owning the unfiltered truth about who you are in Christ. It's time to build something new from the pieces and own the *purpose* within your dirt. Get out of your own way and watch God work!

Confession

I used to wear my brokenness as a badge.

Truth

There is freedom found in building something new.

.

Journal entry
July 15, 2017

Hello,

In order to move forward, I've had to revisit some failure in my life. The more I dig, the more I realize that there's been a pattern of pain following my heart around for too many years. I never saw it before—the hurt that hasn't healed and the defenses I've built up to keep myself from being damaged again.

The girls and I took a trip to Oklahoma last month, and I received a word from a woman named Connie Tousha. I've followed her ministry for many years, and she happened to be doing one of the night services for a meeting my dad was speaking at. Of course, she doesn't know me from Adam, but I was desperate to hear *anything* from God concerning my life.

I've never been that weepy person in church. Sharing emotional moments during worship was one thing, but weeping throughout a service was never something I was known to do. ... But sitting in a pile of tears and Kleenexes seems to be the only thing I'm good for nowadays.

I couldn't tell you what exactly she preached on, but as soon as the altar call came, I was the first one to shoot out of my seat and make my way to the front. I stood in the back of the group so I could blend in with all the extra bodies standing up front. I told God that if he had a word for me, Connie could find me on her own. *I'm angry at life, and I'm doing all I can to just stand up here in the first place.* Lo and behold, not even two minutes of standing in a flood of tears, she made her way through the crowd to stick her long, bony finger in my face.

"You have been through hell and back in your lifetime," she said. "It seems like you've been around the world and through some major *stuff,* but this one thing is true: you know the grace of God in a *huge* way. God is fixing to bring some opportunities to you, and with these opportunities, "kingdom" will be written all over them. ... There's something in your life that's fixing to cause you to let go of something that's been like dead weight to you and your ministry. The anointing is too strong, and where I am going to take you is too big for you to drag that into this next season of your life. People will talk, and honey, let them talk, because what I'm fixing to do will make people stand back and say, 'This had God's hand all over it!' Get ready because the door is swinging open wide, and it is time to move forward!"

I immediately thought to myself, That is not my husband she's talking about! God is not a God of divorce. He wouldn't tell me the one I made a covenant with is like dead weight to my ministry. *Surely there's something else I need to let go of.*

Looking over my life in the past month has allowed me to come face to face with some harsh realities. The biggest one has been this: divorce was not my choice, but this marriage was not God's choice either.

We're presented with choices in life, and, to me, that is one of the many great things about God; he lets us decide what it is that we want for our life ... even if it isn't his best for us. I chose to get married at eighteen years old. I chose not to follow the wisdom of multiple people who said it wasn't God's best for the call I had on my life. I chose to defy God, even when he warned me with dreams to not follow through with the marriage. I chose to make it my life's struggle to always strive for *more* in ministry but to never truly be able to get there, because I didn't choose the right partner.

I have to take responsibility for lowering the standard of purpose on my life by settling for potential. Maybe I wouldn't have settled if I had dealt with areas of my life that had never healed. But either way, I got two beautiful girls out of this life, and I couldn't be more blessed. I couldn't imagine life without them by my side. So, from here, I have to recognize the downfall, repent, and pick myself back up. I have to learn from the lesson and make a vow to do things right from here on out.

My Uncle Joe served in the Vietnam War and shared with me some wisdom that I've been tightly holding on to this past month. With his hand on my shoulder, he looked me in the eye and said, "I fought with soldiers who were my brothers and family. I saw more death than anyone should ever have to experience or see in a lifetime. And we were taught in service to leave no man behind ... unless they were dead. The hardest thing for me to do was to see my brothers die before my eyes, and then willingly leave them behind. But what you need to know is that sometimes you have to *grieve them* and *leave them* in order to survive."

I didn't choose divorce. I chose marriage, even though that wasn't God's best. What I have to do now is learn to "grieve him and leave him" so that I can survive this season of my life.

I know I have more waiting for me up ahead, and I can't wait to find it.

Alissa

Chapter 7: *Breaking Pattern*

The first step in building toward your promise of destiny is to assess the damage of your life. But how do you properly do that? For me, I came to the conclusion that there will always be three main categories when it comes to owning the pieces of my heart:

1. The pieces that others broke.
2. The pieces that I broke.

And then there is what I like to call ...

3. The shatter effect (you broke me, so I will self-destruct).

If you're going to pick yourself up off the floor and build again, you have to meet the requirements—by recognizing where the hurt is coming from—of confronting the areas you've been trying to avoid,. Whether or not you've intentionally shoved things under a rug of filters, the truth is that you won't find your voice again unless you allow yourself to become vulnerable in the valley of life. No one enjoys this part of the process. It's actually a major thing that keeps people from moving forward because allowing yourself to become vulnerable and exposed is not fun. But y'all, it is necessary.

I know I've said this before, but I'm going to say it again. ... Part of owning your truth is being able to take responsibility for the pieces of your life.

Part of owning your truth is being able to take responsibility for the pieces of your life.

Listen, everything against logical explanation would tell you that you should never have to own responsibility for the hurt that someone else put you through when you did nothing to deserve the damage. It's much easier to blame all your wreckage on others, but what if further damage could have been prevented by allowing yourself to unfilter the dirt behind your pain? What if you had actively dealt with it, rather than faking filtered joy to cover it up? How many other hurtful places could you have avoided by owning the truth that it's your responsibility to rebuild and refusing to take painful pieces into other areas and relationships of your life?

For me, the truth behind my marriage failing was ultimately found in my husband's decision to walk away from his family for another woman. I could have placed every bit of responsibility completely on him for breaking our family apart, and many would have agreed with me that the fault was his. But what I found to be true later on, in my process toward promise, was that I had carried the badge of brokenness into our marriage long before we ever said, "I do." And that caused not one category of brokenness, not two, but *all three categories* to take place within our relationship.

I was broken from a previous relationship I had shoved under the rug and never dealt with (category one). When my husband did things that reminded me of that relationship, I would, as a defense mechanism, break him in return to prevent my heart from further hurt (category two). As we continued to damage our relationship (by breaking each other and throwing stones of hurt and pain), I began to see self-destruction take place because I believed the lie that I had gotten what I deserved (category three). And through many different circumstances—like childhood hurts, insecurities, wounds, rejection, words, and loss—that cycle kept repeating itself. Because both of us hadn't dealt with our heart issues, it caused a pattern of breaking to take place in our relationship, and that became our normal.

So many times, we confuse our brokenness for the belief that God is angry at us—and, surely, we're being punished for something we've done wrong in our life. During that season, I believed I wouldn't have experienced the pain of divorce if I wouldn't have settled for someone based upon feelings rather than the well-being of my future. Although that's true—and most certainly could have prevented all the pain my girls and I had to sort through—that thought process planted a lie of brokenness inside my head that lasted for years. That lie said, "You are getting what you deserve. A loveless and hopeless marriage." It left me with the belief system that God was punishing me for disobedience, and that, out of revenge for my actions, he didn't restore my marriage.

Let me unlfilter that lie for you because it's one that has plagued the lives of people for far too long. When I truly began the process of identifying the areas of my life, I was reminded of the dream I had a year prior to the nightmare called divorce. I hadn't read that journal entry since the day I wrote it, but it all began to make perfect sense as I flipped through the pages. "Sometimes I have to swallow up life as you knew it in order to give you the life I always intended for you to have."

Friend, God doesn't allow your life to fall apart out of revenge for disobedience. His heart has always been, and will always be, *for* you and not *against.* The misconception that sin will mark you as a criminal needing punishment from God has got to stop! Jesus' grace screamed from the cross, "I choose to cover you in my love despite all the dirt that has covered up your life." So hear me loud and clear. God is not punishing you for your sin! He is positioning you toward your promise!

Confession #7 : I built a life that God never gave me permission to

build.

In fact, he warned me through multiple leaders, pastors, dreams, and friends that this was not his best for my future. I chose to build a life on a foundation of *potential* instead of *purpose*. And guess what?

It didn't stand. It couldn't hold the weight of promise that was inside the walls of my heart.

That reminds me of a story in the Bible that went a little something like this:

Therefore everyone who hears these words of mine and puts them into practice is like a wise man who built his house on the rock. The rain came down, the streams rose, and the winds blew and beat against that house; yet it did not fall, because it had its foundation on the rock. But everyone who hears these words of mine and does not put them into practice is like a foolish man who built his house on sand. The rain came down, the streams rose, and the winds blew and beat against that house, and it fell with a great crash. (Matthew 7:24-27)

How many times do we do this? How many times do we mistake consequence for being convicted as guilty? How many times do we wipe our hands clean of the choices we've made by putting it off as punishment, instead of recognizing that we're being pointed toward acknowledging our wreckage?

The thing is, taking punishment is easy. Posturing yourself to correct the choices you've made is hard. Are you ready for some unfiltered truth? It's not God's job to keep something from falling apart when he never built it in the first place! Stop blaming him for the destruction of your life. He did not destroy you! Through his love and grace, he has placed you in a position to be delivered out of something that was never yours to build in the first place.

But what if you didn't build anything at all? What if the brokenness came from someone else tearing down the confident, loving, and free person that you were? How do you move on from the pile of pain that's reminding you of the person you used to be? Is it truly your responsibility to take ownership of the pieces when the wreckage came from watching yourself be destroyed?

Friend, the last thing I'd ever want to do is pretend like I know your story. I haven't walked through the dirt you're kicking up right now, and I certainly don't know what it's like to trudge through the mud you've had to navigate on your own. The only story I'm responsible for telling is my own, but I hope that sharing my dirt will help you find some promise hiding in yours.

I don't know if you'll believe me, but the #UNFILTERED truth is that I created thirteen years of track marks in a muddy road I couldn't seem to find my way out of. At fourteen years old, I found myself questioning my beauty, value, and worth ... all because I made a choice. Yep, you read that right. ONE choice altered the course of my life for over a decade, and the story went a little something like this.

Girl meets boy, boy says, "I love you," and girl does just about anything he wants her to—just short of giving him her v-card (virginity). That first relationship in my life started an ongoing cycle of rebellion. It was boy number one that my parents didn't approve of, and somehow, I felt the incessant need to prove them wrong by clinging to him for dear life. So I did what lots of teenagers do—I made the choice to lie.

The plan was to tell my parents I was going to a friend's house to work on a science project. The truth was that I'd meet my boyfriend at his friend's house instead. In just one short evening, I found that one small decision would lead to huge consequences and ultimately place guilt and shame on my shoulders for years. Without knowing it, I'd step into a situation where I was surrounded by familiar faces ... only to learn that they'd concocted a plan to "make me a woman." With some of my best guyfriends guarding the door, I began to live through the scariest hour of my life in a stranger's bathroom.

Would you believe me if I told you that the whole time I was being raped I never once blamed my rapist or the guys who helped make it happen? Would you believe me if I told you that the person I hated the most in that room was myself? Let me tell you, something beyond my virginity was taken from me in that room; my ability to see myself as valuable, worthy, and loved was destroyed. For over ten years after that, I fought my own demons—eating disorders, self-hate, cutting, and depression—and I carried the pain with me as a badge throughout my life.

I don't know why tragic things happen to us, friends; all I know is that sometimes people do evil things. It could be connected to one stupid lie about a science project, or it could just be happenstance. Regardless, I've learned that my destroyer does not determine my destiny. ... I do. The moment I found the courage to face my trauma was the moment I discovered truth lying in the midst of it. The destruction of my life may not have come from my hands, but the destiny built in my life depends solely on my hands.

My destroyer does not determine my destiny.

Let me ask you, what did you build in life that seems to be disintegrating? What pieces are you having to sort through in order to take ownership of the wreckage? What badges from the horrible things that happened to you do you need to put down? How did you get here, and where could you have been wiser?

Your truth may be that you settled for potential instead of purpose, just like me. It could be that you married purpose but allowed destruction to come in by not guarding your vows and covenant correctly. Your truth could be found within fallen friendships and loyalties that were betrayed. Or maybe abuse, rejection, sexual assault of any kind, or tragedy has caused a domino effect of brokenness in your life.

Take a second to pause. Breathe in. Breathe out. Now ask yourself,

Where are the pieces that have fallen, and have I truly taken time out to acknowledge they're there?

Now that you've recognized the pile of rubble that got you to this place in life, what are you going to do about it? Are you going to continue to blame God for destroying your life? Are you going to continue hating him for letting it all fall apart, when he never had a hand in building that version of you in the first place? Will you continue to own your "right to be right" by wearing painful pieces as badges of honor so you can remain the victim of your story? How many times are you going to continue to carry one piece after another into each area of your life before you finally self-destruct and are left with nothing to save?

Stop! You can do better than that! Take ownership of your ability to rebuild, and make sure you build correctly this time around. Protect your purpose by getting up off the ground of defeat and posturing yourself toward promise!

Yes, God may be letting it all fall apart, but have you ever thought that maybe this is where it all begins to fall into place? Your life is not over; it's simply getting in order. This is your opportunity to surrender the pieces into the Father's hands. This is where he can put you back together differently. This is where sharp edges cut away pieces of your character that no longer need to stay. This is where trust is built, and faith becomes a foundation that learns how to stand. This is where pieces that don't fit become a point of reference to remind you of the person you never want to be again. This is where your building ground is. This is your becoming.

Your life is not over; it's simply getting into order.

One of the hardest things you'll ever have to do is grieve the life of someone who's not dead. The closest thing to that is grieving the life you could have had if it all wouldn't have shattered. So today you get to make a choice. You can make a home in the rubble of grief, or you can heal from the pieces by leaving this season with the mindset that you're being rebuilt. You have what it takes ... so stop believing the lies, and—for the love of coffee—own your truth!

Confession

I built a life that God never gave me permission to build.

Truth

God did not destroy you. He has placed you in a position to be delivered out of something that he didn't build.

Journal entry
July 18, 2017

Hello,

I haven't eaten in days.

I haven't slept in days.

So much has taken place. I should have been writing, but honestly, it's difficult writing about the worst time in my life.

But here I am.

I feel like a walking zombie that's been high for far too long … only I haven't been. But my life feels like a drug. It's all become one big haze of nothingness, and I am numb to it all. I don't feel a thing. In fact, I'm pretty sure if you opened my chest up, you wouldn't even find a heart.

Last night was horrendous. It's 10:45 a.m., and I'm just now really getting around. It's all I can do to get out of bed. Somehow, I finally managed to make myself a coffee, and I'm currently forcing myself to at least eat a cup of yogurt.

Shonda called me this morning. She's been counseling me through all this hell. Bless her. Lord knows I didn't need some religious prude to guide me through this nightmare, and I don't think I could have handled having someone require me to wear a mask in order to prove that I can squeeze out one last ounce of faith. But with her and my parents guiding me through, I think I just might make it out alive … I hope.

The truth is, I feel as though I'm walking down a glass-covered road, and I'm doing it barefoot.

There's nothing glamourous about this journey, and I don't need the kind of people in my life who are going to glamorize the scenario with religion and Scripture. Those are not my people right now. They can't help me. The kind of people I need in my corner are the people I don't have to hide my ugly from. The kind of people I can call when I'm out of my mind on anxiety meds. The kind of people whose honor it is to talk me off the ledge when all I want to do is drown myself in a bottle or pick up a gun to end it all. They're the ones who tell me that I'm not crazy for feeling *all* the things. The ones who give me permission to cuss, scream, and break things while I process the emotions of it all. The dear souls who say it's *okay* to be right where I am for a minute. Hurt. Confused. Sad. Angry. Numb.

But they don't leave me there. No, they heal with me.

I ignored Shonda's call twice this morning. I guess my mom was concerned for me—and shared her worries with Shonda—since I haven't gotten out of bed in a week and have officially stopped taking calls from my parents, unless it concerns getting help with my kids. But I finally answered when call number three began to ring in—the view of my ceiling, paired with the vibration of my phone cutting through the silence in my house, became too much for me to handle.

"Hello," I answered, with no enthusiasm in my voice.

"Hey, sweet girl. How are you doing?"

Silence.

"Listen, your mom called me, and I need you to know that you don't have to fight this alone, baby girl."

Silence.

"Alissa, it's okay to *feel*, sweetheart. Don't push it away and shut it out. You are not wrong for feeling all the emotions under the sun right now. Do you hear me? You don't have to be scared to feel."

Silence.

"You don't even have to say anything. I'm right here as long as you need me."

I've never experienced it before, but somehow, the lump in my throat had stolen the sound of my voice, and that numb feeling I'd been fighting for days seemed to have locked all my words away in a box around my neck. As tears streamed down my face, all she could hear were soft sobs coming from the other end of the line. And what happened next was like much-needed healing balm for my heart. It medicated me. It soothed the painful areas. It helped me to breathe a little deeper and find some sound to my voice.

"Sweet girl," she started, "don't say anything. Just listen to me as I read from Psalm 27. Listen to it as I read it with your name inserted because, honey, this is your promise right now.

'The Lord is Alissa's light and her salvation—whom shall she fear? The Lord is Alissa's refuge and the fortress of her life—whom shall she dread? When the wicked came against her to eat up her flesh, her adversaries and her enemies, they stumbled and fell. Though an army encamp against her, her heart will not fear; though war arise against her, even in this she is confident.'"

All I could do was lie there. No words could be found in that moment, and even though she couldn't hear me, I thanked her for not choking me on Scripture or forcing me to wear a mask that said, "I am okay." All I needed in that moment was the Word given to me gracefully and with love.

She continued:

"Sweet girl, I want you to give me your top three things that you're afraid of right now. Don't even think of it too long. Just tell me three things that are keeping you in bed and unable to move."

It took everything in me to let those three things out of my mouth, but despite the tangible pain I felt while lying in my bed, I managed to find enough strength to say, "Forever alone ... worthless ... unlovable."

"Listen to the rest of this chapter sweetheart, 'One thing I have asked of the Lord, and that I will seek: That I may dwell in the house of the Lord (his presence) all the days of my life, to gaze upon the beauty of the Lord and to meditate in his temple. For in the day of trouble, through this divorce, he will hide me in his shelter; in the secret place of his tent he will hide me; he will lift me up on a rock. And now my head will be lifted up above my enemies that are around me and the fear of being forever alone, worthless, and unlovable. In his tent, I will offer sacrifices with shouts of joy; I will sing, yes, I will sing praises to the Lord."

It was simple. It's what some would even label as common sense.

I've been paralyzed with fear and pain. I've been plastered to my bed and wrapped up in depression, the occasional anxiety pill, and thoughts of hopelessness. But all it took was someone taking the time to read the Word over me when I couldn't find the willpower to do it myself. It cracked my chest wide open. It shifted something inside my spirit. It transported me into a real-life version of *Grey's Anatomy* as Shonda screamed, "Code blue!" in the spirit and got the crash cart out. It brought me back to life while I listened to her read over me.

She challenged me to find Scripture that combats these three fears head-on, and then to declare them over myself. I agreed. I need to continue to collect them and allow them to medicate my heart. It's been hard, but I have to believe that somehow, through this unbearable pain, there is unbelievable purpose waiting on the other side.

Alissa

Chapter 8: *Feel*

I had the opportunity to meet up with a sweet lady at the cutest little coffee shop in downtown Savannah. It was the kind of shop that served the most delicious coffee in the cutest little mugs, but also had the side hustle of a nice, tall glass of wine. The vibe was laid back—with a small, but on-point, bakery where they encourage you to pick your poison for the day—and they offered a menu with all the best things to treat yourself to for lunch.

The seating had cozy little spots where sweet memories could be made, and sections for businesspeople to grind out a project for their upcoming deadline. As I sat there waiting for my friend to show up, I thought to myself how that was a picture of what the church should look like. It should be a place where people can come, no matter what their personal pace, style, or need is, and walk out of those doors feeling one thing: refreshed.

As we sat in that magical, little place, we began to discuss tragedy, pain, trauma, and what the restoration process looked like in both of our lives. One story after another was shared, and it all looked like this: I grew up in church; she didn't. She waited until her late twenties to get married; I entered my first marriage at the age of eighteen. She found relationship with Jesus two years ago and started serving; I said the salvation prayer at age five and was raised in ministry. I've given birth to two healthy babies; she's miscarried twins. I've been through divorce as an adult; she's was the victim of divorce as a child. Her teen years were wrapped up in parties and covering up her parents' mess; my teen years were wrapped up in eating disorders, rape, and running from God.

We found that although our stories were incredibly different, both of us agreed that our solution was undeniably the same. Our processes took two disparate paths, but the promise standing behind them had the same destination.

For so long I felt like the church defined restoration as "one size fits all": So you cheated on your spouse? Here's our restoration process. So you're dealing with suicidal thoughts? Let me point you in the direction of restoration. So you're addicted to porn, drugs, or alcohol? Our restoration process is right over here. So you're grieving the loss of a loved one? Restoration is this way. So you just can't seem to get life together, and you're on the brink of the biggest possible meltdown the world has ever seen? Please follow me toward the same, exact restoration process that we filter every, single person through, no matter what they're facing. (I wish you could see the eye roll I'm giving as I type this out.) And—for the love of coffee—please make the madness stop!

Yes! Restoration is a process.

No! Restoration is not a magical pill (or prayer) that works the same way for all people and all scenarios. Every situation is different, and every person and personality is unique. The way I process emotions, trauma, and healing could differ from the way you approach it. There is no one-size-fits-all technique, strategy, or program when it comes to restoring the human heart. The only thing that should remain the same is the name of Jesus and his Word.

Friend, restoration is not a one-size-fits-all plan of strategy, but it is (and will always be) a one-size-fits-all *promise* that's available for everyone to receive. If you allow yourself to take the journey, by going through a process that holds nothing back and covers nothing up, you'll see destiny grow in your life.

If I've learned anything along the way, it's that this process is a journey that never ends. That's the reality of it. Life is an equal-opportunity offender and will always surprise you with unfortunate events along the way.

Next month will mark two years since I sat down in that smoky room across from a ballsy lawyer who allowed me to see hope from a much different perspective. It was the day my whole life began to fall apart in order to fall into place. If I could take the woman I was by the hand, I'd remind her that sometimes things have to unravel so that you can become unfiltered. I would tell her that her *now* is necessary for her *tomorrow*. I would reassure her that, even through her pain, this is the day each answered prayer will find its way to her doorstep.

I'm a much different woman now, and in a much different place in life. My heart has learned to live from a place of wholeness, and my mind has learned to focus forward by not living backward. Owning my truth, unfiltered, has become a process I've taught myself to practice. The trick has been to embrace *posture* more than *perfection*. I might not ever become perfect in owning my DNA and the truth of who God has called me to be, but if I become a professional at posturing myself toward the destiny he has for my life—no matter what hell I may face along the way—then I cannot fail.

Confession #8: I used to think "faith" meant being numb to

feeling.

As I write this chapter, I'm currently sitting in my two-story house in front of the fireplace, enjoying a nice cup of hot coffee. I'm now living in Savannah, Georgia with the man whose last name I found true purpose in. We've been married a little over a year, and I can confidently say that he's the answer to every prayer I ever prayed for my ex-husband to become, and he is so much more than I ever knew I wanted (or needed) in my life. (I'll be covering more of our story, in depth, during Part 2 of this book.)

Today we got news that should change everything, but my spirit sings "your promise still stands." I'm reminded of the day that I wrote one of the hardest journal entries of my life. It was Kinsleigh's seventh birthday and I had just met with a divorce attorney. Today is a day after Aurora's seventh birthday. And both times, I just so happened to be writing in journals with the same scripture, Proverbs 3:5, inscribed on the front, "Trust in the Lord with all your heart."

I'm still learning that lesson as I walk out my destiny—and I even struggled sharing that with you in this book—but the title is #*Unfiltered*, and this is currently my truth.

This morning I got a call that Bran and I have been waiting to receive; the one that was supposed to be another check mark by "all things good" and put us one step closer to growing our little family. Right after we got married, we almost immediately made the decision to try for a baby. I always wanted more kids, and Bran has always had a heart to be a daddy. Of course, he sees my girls as his own, but that doesn't change the desire for a child who carries Holt blood. And with the girls growing so fast, we decided that we'd jump on into family growth and make the Holt family bigger. So for ten straight months we tried, with no such luck, before deciding it was time for both of us to get checked out. We wanted to be sure there was nothing to be concerned about, and if there was, we wanted to know how to direct our faith and prayers.

It's funny how God knew I'd be writing this chapter today, because my morning started off with all kinds of feels and the challenge to posture myself in faith toward promise. It was 8:45 when my phone rang this morning. Through my yawn and morning voice, I answered the phone,

"Hello."

A perky woman on the other end of line replied, "Hi Alissa! This is Sarah from Dr. Jackson's office. I have the results from your husband's tests here and was calling to give you the report."

"Ok, let's hear it."

Everything became a blur from that point forward. I turned over in bed, watching my husband sleep peacefully, while I listened to this woman share with me instructions, concerns, surgery options, and more testing we'd need to follow through with. The diagnosis was not one that many people would label as "good," but it was also not labeled as "without hope."

She went on, "The report showed that there's a decrease in sperm count, and mobility is not as good as we would hope. Please follow through with the instructions we would like for him to do, and we'll need him to follow up with us in three months. As for you, we want to proceed forward with your surgery next month. We'll be checking for scar tissue from your c-sections and will also remove any signs of endometriosis while we're in there. This will give you a better chance of pregnancy."

"Okay ... thank you."

As soon as I hung up the phone, Bran sat up in bed, "Who was that?"

My head was still spinning as it tried to process the information. "Dr. Jackson's office with your results."

His eyes popped open with concern as he searched my face for answers, "What'd they say?"

I paused, stretched, and asked God to give me wisdom and strength in how I delivered the news. ... I knew Bran would need me. As I began to tell him the results, I watched the man I love more than life break right in front of my eyes.

Looking your husband in the face and confirming one of his deepest fears is probably one of the hardest things I've ever had to do, without a doubt. As I began to spill the news to him, in the gentlest way I possibly could, I turned to find him silently sobbing into his pillow with fear. What do you do when there's nothing to do? What do you say when there's nothing to say? How do you react when the thing you've been praying and believing for turns into pain as you wait for your promise?

Let me ask you, what is it that you're confronted with today? Is it divorce or infertility? Is it depression or suicidal thoughts? Is it loss or failure? Is it disease or poverty? I'm there with you, my friend. I feel the struggle of posturing myself toward promise today. But guess what?

I am here ... writing this book from the position of promise because I know that we can own our destiny despite the things life throws our way! It's right under my feet. Right here in the dirt. ... I just have to dig.

In that moment, I remembered the phone call with Shonda, and how it washed over my heart with peace. I held on to all the nights where my Dad had offered me an ear to hear my pain and a shoulder to carry the burden. I took a second to remember the healing that comes in feeling the reality of where you are in a moment of hurt and allowing it to become your ministry of worship to God through your tears.

If going through divorce taught me anything in life, it's that the answer isn't always what the heart needs to hear. Sometimes what the heart *needs* is an ear to hear what it has to say for once. Sometimes the best thing to do in the valley of a painful moment is to listen and not voice an opinion. So that's what I did. I listened to my husband. I listened to his fears and watched his pain cut through his tears as he began to share with me a piece of his heart that was severely wounded in that moment. Even though his words went against the promise of a growing family. Even though they questioned God's faithfulness. Even though they stole his worth, value, and the truth of who he is as a man ... I listened. I knew his heart had to feel before it could heal, and I knew my words couldn't fix his pain. The only thing that could ease it would be my willingness to listen. That's where the grace and love of Jesus is found, right there in the dirt.

I wish I could tell you that we've snapped out of it this morning. I wish I could say that the moment I heard the nurse tell me the report, it didn't move or shake my faith. I wish I could write about how the news didn't wound my husband's heart or cause us to feel hopeless. But I can't, and you know what? That's okay.

Faith doesn't mean you're numb to feeling. Faith means your feelings don't determine your trust that God can, and will, work all things together for your good (see Romans 8:28, AMP). It means that through the pain, hurt, and wounds, you can trust him with all the grief in your heart and lean not on your own understanding. It means you can remain confident (despite the pain) that you will see the goodness of the Lord (see Psalm 27:13).

Faith doesn't mean you're numb to feeling.

So hear me as I say this: *feeling* doesn't cancel out your faith! Feelings are the substance you trust the Father with. It's what you place into the dirt of that moment while you rely on the hope of Jesus to bring something dead back to life. It's the place where pain is turned into purpose and promise becomes a posture. Foundation begins to be laid when you trust him there and don't avoid the process of feeling.

I was raised in the Word of Faith movement all my life. My parents graduated from Rhema Bible Training Center in 1985, and I followed in their footsteps by graduating in 2009. In case you aren't sure of the reputation this school has to offer, it was founded by the leading "father" of the Word of Faith movement, Kenneth E. Hagin. So, as you can imagine, faith was not a foreign concept to me, and knowing how to speak, believe, and see promise was a common practice of mine. I memorized and quoted scriptures like this when I couldn't see the reality of promise in my life:

Now faith is the substance of things hoped for, the evidence of

things not seen. (Hebrews 11:1, NKJV)

I wrote this scripture on my mirror when I felt like I was weak in my walk with God:

So then faith comes by hearing, and hearing by the word of God.

(Romans 10:17, NKJV)

I reminded myself of this verse when I felt like salvation could be stolen by the dirt in my life:

For by grace you have been saved through faith, and that not of yourselves; it is the gift of God. (Ephesians 2:8, NKJV)

I stood on these words when I felt like my will and belief system were too small to make a difference:

He replied, "Because you have so little faith. Truly I tell you, if you have faith as small as a mustard seed, you can say to this mountain, 'Move from here to there,' and it will move. Nothing will be impossible for you." (Matthew 17:20)

All these scriptures (and so many more) were staples in my walk with God. They carried me though some of my darkest seasons and brought me life when I wasn't sure how I could possibly go on. What I found is that there will always be a lie that tries to follow every truth; if we aren't careful, we can buy into the belief that this is accurate, when it's nothing more than a trap to keep you from living a life of freedom in Christ.

The lie I want to unfilter for you is the idea that *faith* means being numb to *feeling*. So many times, I've felt like I had to deny the reality of my life in order to remain in faith that God was working out the details.

When my husband left me, I lived in a house where the toilet was falling through the floor, rooms would flood when it rained, there was no heat in the winter, and the animal who lived under my bedroom floor became the sound I fell asleep to every night. I had to apply for food stamps and visit food banks to feed my babies, and your girl was on all the things the government could provide to make ends meet.

One day, I made a statement in passing, saying, "I guess the girls and I will be eating rice and gravy all week because I have to buy toilet paper instead of groceries."

A member of our church heard me and began to scold me all of a sudden, "Ok now, woman of faith! Believe what you receive! Speak it into existence, and you won't have any money or any extra food, just like you said!"

I immediately felt guilt and shame for talking about my reality. If I couldn't verbalize my truth to the people I serve God with, then who could I find freedom in talking to? That was the reality of my life, right? Promise wasn't anywhere in sight. Do you ignore the truth of where you are in those moments?

For most of my life, I've been led to believe that feelings are fatal to my faith. I was taught that verbalizing my reality (and the worries or concerns that come with it) could somehow cancel out the promise of God for my life. And that left me with the mindset that I must shove all my feelings under a rug of filters or else I'm not the woman of faith I claim to be.

That is a lie, y'all!

Faith without feeling is destructive! It denies you the ability to uproot the issue that's keeping the promise from being planted in your life. Avoiding the facts of your life will keep you from facing the giant that's in your way. David didn't deny the obstacle that was in front of him. He confronted it face to face by planting himself in the soil of the situation. And by doing so, he was able to embrace his destiny as he dug in the dirt and found the stones that made the enemy fall. The stones in your dirt can signify the hard places you keep trying to cover up. What if allowing yourself to embrace the stones (trauma, pain, rejection, abuse, loss) causes them to tangibly become the thing you use to take down the giant you're trying to defeat?

Allowing myself to *feel* in faith gave my pain permission to become substance. It brought me to a place where I not only planted myself within the dirt of my life, but I began to see the evidence of *promise* grow in front of me.

Now faith is the substance of things hoped for, the

evidence of things not seen. (Hebrews 11:1, NKJV)

Allowing myself to feel in faith gave my pain

permission to become substance.

Hope[1]

ˈhōp

noun

1. A feeling of expectation and desire for a certain thing to happen

Friends, you cannot have faith without feeling, because feeling is the substance that brings forth the evidence of promise in your life, even if you can't see it right now. Stop allowing yourself to dismiss the reality of how you feel. That could be what's keeping you from walking in the fullness of what faith truly is. Maybe faith comes with the courage to embrace the stones while declaring the truth of his Word and promise by believing he is in control.

Today we're learning to continue the process toward promise, and I did that by allowing Bran to feel. I know this will bring us face to face with the faith we need to see a son come forth. This battle will result in a baby.

I feel the hope of healing as I stand in the soil and use these hard moments to confront the lie that tells me that my God is not big enough. I will watch life grow inside me and the lie of infertility fall in front of me. All I have to do is use these hard moments as stones to sling toward my destiny.

Confession

I used to think *faith* meant being numb to *feeling*.

Truth

Feeling doesn't cancel out your faith. Feelings are the substance you trust the Father with.

.

Journal entry

July 26, 2017

Hello,

Happy ME day! I'm twenty-eight years young, and man, do I feel like life has dealt me a handful. Brian Courtney Wilson's song "I'll Just Say Yes" just came on Pandora as I sit here at my aunt's house. It couldn't be more perfect timing, because this is how I feel. God, I'll just say yes to twenty-eight. Yes, to this new season. Yes, to all you have for me.

Last night I said a prayer as I got ready for bed. "God, I thank you for where I've been, but I thank you more for where I'm going. I refuse to wallow in self-pity and allow the circumstances of my life to kill my destination."

This is my first birthday without my husband, but instead of sulking, I want to make a list of declarations for my life:

I declare that twenty-eight is going to be great! Twenty-eight is the year I'll meet my mate. Twenty-eight has no more weight, and I'll no longer have to wait for the promise of God on my life. It's the year to create the life God has always had for me to live. I declare that twenty-eight will be the year my future will no longer be on debate. It's the year I locate my place called "There." Twenty-eight is the year I'm on a mandate from God. It's the year I can relate to his heart and understand my design and purpose on a different level. I declare that it's a new season and I'm simply on rotate.

As I looked up the number twenty-eight this morning, I found that its meaning has significance. In Hebrew Gematria, *koakh*—meaning "power" and "energy"—is the word that corresponds to the number twenty-eight. Twenty-eight is also the number of Hebrew letters in Genesis 1:1 which reads, "In the beginning God *created* the heavens and earth" (emphasis added).

I feel like life has turned over on me, but God is saying, You're just on rotate. Your world feels like it's spinning, but I'm just positioning you in a way that allows you to rotate around me. I'm putting you on display so that people can watch me create a *new* thing; a thing that will not only change you but will also change them.

I believe, from the depths of my soul, that this is not a *loss*; it has been God setting me up for a *launch*. This is the year that I'm being put on display to rotate around God as he creates something that people will watch from a distance. This is where all my chaos will meet his creation.

This is where all my chaos will meet his

creation.

Father, create in me a new thing (see Psalm 51:10, MSG). Open my ears, unlock my mouth, lift my eyes, guide my feet, take my hand, and speak to my heart. Allow me to remain faithful and pure, and above all, please keep me obedient. For once in my life, I belong to no man, and I need help to remain focused on you and your future for me. Please don't let me down. Show me what true love is like.

Last night I had a dream that had me wishing I never would have woken up. I don't know if it's just the fact that this is my first celebration after filing for divorce, or if this is a reminder that God is putting things in order.

In the dream, I was on a date and surprised that it wasn't with my current husband. We were eating at an uber fancy place, and I was dressed in a gorgeous gown. The man across from me wore a suit and was undeniably handsome. I couldn't see his facial features, but I remember his smile, dark hair, and that he was tall and bigger in stature. While we sat there, we were asking about each other's dreams, aspirations, likes, and dislikes.

He said, "Forgive me. I'm a questions guy," and truly seemed genuine in getting to know me.

I remember the connection between us because it was almost like we were instant best friends. Our ministry goals, music desires, family wants, and our heart for Jesus were so on-point with each other that I remember feeling in my gut, "This is it."

Then all of a sudden, he looked at me and said, "I might be crazy for saying this, but where have you been my whole life? I think I might just make you my wife."

I just knew he was supposed to be my husband, and I know it sounds insane, but I believe I will find this man!

And to my surprise, this morning Rory came to me and said, "Mommy, last night I had a dream that I was hugging my new daddy. Daddy was there in a red shirt, and I thought it was Dada, but I was hugging my *new* daddy." I breathed a fresh breath of hope knowing that I can trust God with my daughters, and that they're going to be okay. He's working it out, and I am confident that his promise is true. This will be a year of dreams come true.

Alissa

Chapter 9: Create

My youngest daughter is a creative heart. She makes her Barbie dolls bunk beds out of random supplies like shoe boxes, straws, and tape, and creates backpacks from duct tape and old, tie-dye maxi skirts. I don't quite know where she gets the ideas or how she became such a creative genius. I like to think she inherited that gene from me, but I'm pretty sure I never could have figured out how to build an airplane out of water bottles, cardboard, and hot glue.

As I watch her gather supplies, cut things up, make messes, and construct something out of nothing, I'm reminded of how our destiny looks in the Father's hands. A handful of random circumstances, a pile of messy work, and the touch of a creative God to form destiny out of dirt.

The mark on your life doesn't come from the filth; it comes from the freedom you have to create something beautiful out of that filth.

One week before my husband walked out on me, I received a word from God in Pensacola, Florida. We were on vacation to attend the wedding of one of my best friends. She was the current worship leader at Brownsville Church, so we decided to attend service and check it out. I wasn't expecting anything. And to be completely honest, we were forty minutes late because we were fighting the entire way there. It was our last day of vacation, and he made it crystal clear to me that he didn't want to spend it at church. Regardless, we went, even though we were both mad as bulls and fashionably late.

As soon as we walked into the sanctuary, it became clear to me that this was a unique service. There was no preaching that day. All the service consisted of was worship and the freedom to experience the love of God.

We sat on the far, right-hand side (all the way in the back) so we wouldn't draw attention to ourselves. Both of us were embarrassed to have shown up so late, and the last thing we wanted was a bunch of eyes on the "new people." But I don't guess it mattered much because before I knew it, the pastor stood on the stage and pointed out into the crowd, "The couple in the back ... will you both come here? I need to pray for you. God has given me a word."

We were shocked and looked around sheepishly to make sure it was us that he was talking to. But, sure enough, we made our way to the stage—still angry at each other and reluctant about being there.

With a hand on my shoulder and tears in his eyes, the pastor began to speak over me, "Young lady, there is a season of completion that God is bringing you into. I see that you've been weary, but I see a staff like Moses' that God is placing in your hand. You are being strengthened today for the ministry that you've been called to. You will sing songs of deliverance and minister with a heart for people. When you open your mouth, miracles and healing will take place, and everything you ever dreamt of will begin to come into completion this year."

About that time, his wife looked at me and said, "Do you want a baby? I see a baby in your future."

My desire was always to have more kids, but my husband at the time was done with growing a family. Immediately, he shook his head in disbelief and replied, "No. No more kids for us!"

But then she looked me in the eyes and said, "I'm sorry, hun, but there's a baby coming. I see it clearly and know that you will conceive another child."

Seven days later, I found that those words brought more pain to my life than they did promise. I immediately began to fight the idea that the pastors who spoke over me were false prophets and that God was a liar. How could the year possibly end with completion when my husband was leaving me? How could there possibly be a baby in my future when I had no spouse?

Regardless, I clung to that word and spoke it over myself daily. I reminded God of the promise he gave my heart when that pastor said that everything I ever dreamt of would begin to come into completion that year and that a baby was in my future. It was a daily choice to place before my eyes the vision of promise by putting my voice on it and declaring it every single day, without fail.

Let me tell you, friend, I had no idea that I would see completion take place in my life on the very last day of that same year, just as God said it would. As the clock struck midnight, the Times Square Ball dropped, and people screamed "Happy New Year!" I watched a man of purpose get down on one knee and ask my girls' permission for mommy to be his wife. I was immediately overwhelmed with joy and silently thanked God for keeping his promise (even down to the last minute) by allowing my dreams to come true and completion to take place.

With the promise of a baby still to come, and a ministry that allows me to travel the world singing songs of freedom and speaking about a faithful Father, I can boldly say that holding strong to the promise got me through the pain, and I know God will never fail.

My daddy, Kevin Powers, is one of the most accurate prophets I've ever sat under in ministry. He teaches something I've held on to my entire life, and it's what helped me turn the tables of divorce, defeat, and destruction by changing the game and owning my truth. This bit of wisdom will empower you with the tools you need to no longer make excuses. It allows you to become the engineer behind the hand of God as you help him create something new for your life. Are you ready? It's as simple as this question: What if I told you that you don't have a beginning unless you have a word?

You don't have a beginning unless you have a word.

In the beginning was the *Word*, and the *Word* was with God, and the *Word* was God. (John 1:1, NKJV, emphasis added)

Hear that, guys! You can do all the digging, dirt embracing, trust building, piece sorting, and faith feeling that you want to do, but the reality is that if you don't have a word to stand on then you don't have a starting line. I decided, before my divorce was ever finalized, to be a VOICE and not a VICTIM. I began to speak out about the faithfulness of God before I ever saw an ounce of hope in my life. I did it because I refused to wear broken badges any longer, and I knew that God couldn't build a backbone within me unless there was something to build off of.

One of the questions I receive the most is, "How do you know where to start, and how do you begin if you've never received a personal word from the Lord?" Well, friend, it's simple. You search through the pages of a book that's been kissed with promise for your life. His Word is the best beginning you could ever give yourself, and it comes with the pretzel tie that it will not fail. When I was lying in bed, unable to move and without hope, Shonda called me with words from a book that's been around for thousands of years. And it wasn't a "thus saith the Lord" that got me out of bed; it was a word that had already been spoken and was available and waiting for me long before I ever went through that valley.

Listen. Sometimes you have to stop waiting for God to speak, and instead realize that he has already spoken. I know the feeling of despair and desperation as you beg and plead with God for answers, but what if he's remaining silent because your answer has already been recorded? What if he's just waiting for you to read the promise for yourself?

I received an Instagram message from a follower of mine several months after my divorce took place. She had followed my ministry for years and had watched me voice my victory while I was still a victim, as I spoke life over others who were in the same position as me. She mentioned in her message that I shouldn't make blanket statements about healing from divorce and moving on from pain, because it could trivialize what people have gone through. She stated that not every divorce is alike, and that I was blessed to be raised in a Christian home that taught me how to walk in the Word. She said that many people haven't had that luxury, and some could be offended by my message.

My response to her was that I agreed. Not all divorce is the same, and not every situation will mirror another. I would be foolish to think my experience is yours, and I would be even more ignorant to think my process is a one-size-fits-all plan of healing. But I do know that no matter what the tragedy was that caused you to break (divorce, abandonment, rape, molestation, abuse, poverty, mental illness, disease, loss, and so on), God is still the same God. It doesn't matter what the situation is. What matters is that the solution remains the same ... yesterday, today, and forever.

Pain is pain, y'all, and hurt is hurt. It doesn't matter how big or how small the wound may be; the reality of how that trauma affects your life is, without a doubt, real. I don't dismiss that. I don't deny the truth behind your heartbreak. But what I'm here to help you understand is that *purpose* was breathed into your dirt long before pain ever had the opportunity to mark your life. Your inheritance is to live from a whole heart. When Christ hung on the cross, he sealed that promise thousands of years before your heart ever had a chance to break. You are the answer to the restoration in your life, and you are the one who determines whether destiny comes to pass in your future.

Confession #9: I stole years of destiny from myself by *waiting* instead of *creating*.

Sometimes, in order to move forward, you must be willing to go back to the beginning. The key is to build from the pieces, but the problem is that so many people end up making a bed out of the pain instead. If you want to see progress, you can't stop before you start and then expect God to do all the work! The promise of his Word does not mean that you have no part. His promise is available for you to possess, but, friend, the Word is clear when it says faith without works is dead. There is a building process that must take place.

In the beginning God created the heavens and the earth. (Genesis 1:1)

When we look at the Scriptures, we see two things about our beginning:

1. It starts with a word.
2. Words create.

Before we can move any further in this book, I need to unfilter the lie that says it's our job to wait and God's job to create. In all areas of our life, we understand there's a part we must play in order to create a future for ourselves. If we want to lose weight, we understand the process it takes—diet and exercise—to achieve our goals. If we want a career, we understand the process it takes to earn the degree we need to get that job. If we want to have kids, we understand the process required to bring that child into our life.

Every area of success in our life is preceded by a process of creation. What makes us think that the same doesn't apply when it comes to our destiny and the promise of God? My daddy says it the best when he teaches about this subject, "Prophecy is not predictive; it is creative." God is not *predicting* your future when he gives you the words of his book to stand on. And the people he placed in your life with a word of hope are not palm readers predicting what God has for your life.

"Prophecy is not predictive; it is creative."

Everything God created in the beginning of time was preceded by a word. Nowhere in Genesis does it say that God predicted creation, but what it does say is that God spoke creation. Chapter one of Genesis shows us nine times where "God says" and creation takes place. So here's the deal. Your beginning starts once you receive a word from God. That word can be found in the pages of his book and the promises he says are ours. It can be received by the spiritual leadership in your life that confirms the truth of his Word to your heart. It can be discovered during a personal moment between you and the Father. But whatever the case may be, one thing still stands: Prophecy is not prediction; it is creation.

I've seen people curse God, and those he sent with a word of truth, so many times because the word (promise, destiny, call, or vision) they received never came to pass in their life. Listen, I've been there! I've accused people of "missing God," all because the word they shared didn't line up to my current situation in life. But y'all, there's so much more to destiny than what you see in front of you.

Oftentimes, we believe that once a word is received, or read in the Bible, it's fully God's responsibility to make it happen in our lives. That could not be further from the truth. In fact, that's a lie that has been believed for far too long, and we've got to start taking ownership for our part so that *promise* can become a destination instead of remaining a dream. Stop waiting on the word to happen and start allowing a creation process to take place in your life. If you're the soil that determines what seeds take growth in your life, then you hold the power over what words—good or bad, promise or curse—manifest in your reality. What is it that you're speaking over yourself? What is it that you believe you can have for your life? What is it that you meditate on the most?

He touched their eyes and said, "Become what you believe."

(Matthew 9:29, MSG)

You'll become what you believe you are. You'll receive what you believe you can have. The number one place the enemy will try to mess with is your mind. If he can get you to believe a lie then he can distort your belief system, and if he can distort your belief system then he can alter your entire destiny.

You determine where you go in life by deciding what you believe about yourself!

Your thought life will begin to roll off your tongue if you think on it long enough, and there is life and death in the power of your tongue (see Proverbs 18:21). Your words will plant seeds that either poison your promise or position it for growth. What are you doing to nurture the creative process for the promise to become a reality? Are you walking through dirt and embracing your destiny, or are you making a bed in the pile of wreckage?

On my twenty-eighth birthday, I decided to make a declaration for my life that I spoke over myself every single morning for an entire year. I took every word I'd received from the mouths of spiritual leaders and wrote them out so I could keep them before my eyes. I made a collection of Bible verses that spoke truth over the areas of my life that had been owned by lies for far too long and posted them on my mirror. I made lists of declarations that I spoke over myself daily, and I put together a checklist of what I wanted, needed, and desired in a future husband so that I could lay hands on it each day and pray over him.

I can't tell you that I didn't encounter bad days. I can't tell you that I didn't live through moments where I had to feel in order to heal and allow God to sort through the pieces with me so that I could build. But what I can say is that I had to allow a creative process to take place in my life for me to see the promise come to pass. I had to *stop* waiting, and I had to *start* creating.

As the old saying goes, you do what you can, and God will do what you can't. I had to realize that I couldn't live forward by looking backward. I had to stop dwelling on the past while expecting the future to be in my mouth.

I had to stop dwelling on the past while expecting the future to be in my mouth.

You guys, seeds stop cycles in your life. When a man plants a seed inside a woman, the first sign of creation taking place is that her cycle stops. The promise of that baby takes time to develop, and guess what? No one is angry at God for the nine-month timespan of preparation! There's an understanding that there will be discomfort, stretching, sacrifice, growth, labor pain, and birthing in order for that life to take its first breath. It's not a pretty process, but there's purpose in it. In order for the cycle of hurt, rejection, brokenness, loss, abandonment, etc., to stop in your life, you have to allow the seed of promise to be planted, and you have to stop being angry at God for the waiting and discomfort you experience while you're being positioned.

You may have been marked by dirt, and that's okay. Dirt provides you with the opportunity to plant purpose in your life and stop the cycle that's been on repeat for too long. Take ownership of your life and allow the creative process to take you to your place called "There." Your now is vital for your tomorrow. What are you doing with this season of your life? What do you believe about it? It's time to start speaking truth over the dark areas so that you can watch God create.

Confession

I stole years of destiny from myself by *waiting* instead of *creating*.

Truth

Prophecy is not predictive; it is creative.

Part 2

Walking Through Dirt

Journal entry
July 30, 2017

Hello,

I woke up this morning with a notification from Facebook, and when I clicked it, I was given an option to see memories of what I'd posted "this day" from previous years. It showed that one year ago our little family was complete with the four of us; we were enjoying a night out on the town for dinner, and we all looked so happy. My memory from two years ago showed a picture of us holding a conference at our church in Texas; we were surrounded by people who I thought would always be in my life, and our hearts were full of ministry and growth.

Scrolling through those memories left me with one thought, My, how a lot can change in a year. From Texas to Arkansas, and new journeys to divorce … each year has brought more pain than I can handle.

Then all of a sudden, I heard the Holy Spirit say, *Oh, but how much*

I can restore in a year. Do you trust me?

So with Google to the rescue, I took a second to type in the search bar: "things God can do in a year." I don't know what prompted me to do it, but curiosity took me by surprise … and the results left me a promise.

The first thing to pop up on the screen included stats behind the history of the flood that took place in the Bible. Those stats said that God used a time span of approximately one year to destroy everything and then renew everything by sealing it with a promise. I've read the story about Noah and the flood many times in my life. As a child, I helped my Sunday school teacher by placing the animals on the giant felt board as they entered the ark. Today, I saw the rainbow of promise over my life as I read this story from a new perspective. That promise gives me hope that this storm will not end me, and my dream is starting to make more sense.

"Sometimes I have to swallow up life as you knew it in order to give you the life I always intended for you to have."

If I could put a picture to what God was speaking to my heart, it would look like the story of Noah. He was entrusted with the responsibility to carry purpose through the flood, and though he obeyed, he watched life as he knew it die before his eyes. I wish I couldn't relate to him. I wish I could say that carrying purpose brings a picture of beauty and joy, but the reality is that sometimes things must die so that they can be reborn. Before God could recreate, he had to kill off the life everyone knew. So Noah knows how I feel right about now. My whole world has been ripped out from underneath my feet, and I'm trying desperately to keep my head above water. I'm carrying the words of promise that God has spoken to my heart, but I'm also waiting anxiously for the door to swing open wide so I can release them back into the world.

It is here that I must decide if this storm will be my stopping point or my shifting point. How I steward this will determine whether I'm destroyed in the depths of the circumstances or whether I'm deployed into my place called "There."

As I search through the Bible, I find people who had opportunity to let life destroy them but, instead, they chose to allow it to deploy them. Noah went from floods to favor. David went from hiding in mountains to being heir to a throne. Joseph went from slavery to supremacy. Ruth went from watching a husband die to watching a husband bring destiny to her life. Hannah and Sarah went from barren to blessed. Abigail went from having a wicked husband to having a worthy husband. Each of these people used their storm as opportunity instead of opposition. It led to their destiny and not their destruction. What I'm learning is that God can't take me to the place I'm meant to be unless I go through a testing of my character. What would have happened if these men and women were given their destiny before it was ready to be displayed? How would their story have ended?

The one common denominator I see in the life of every person who God used in great ways was not their lack of dirt; it was their ability to take a journey of discipleship so that they could see their promise. They remembered who they were no matter how bad the storm got, and they didn't let it dictate to them how they believed—they simply became the storm themselves.

I have to become the thunder and lighting. I have to realize that I have the power inside me, through the Holy Spirit, to ride these waves out and see that power become my weapon. I have to realize that although I can be detected on the enemy's radar, I will no longer be the one taking cover … he will.

Alissa, you are the storm. You will no longer drown in pain. You will dance in purpose. You will chart the course and overcome. You will look back one year from now and see that everything might have died, but everything God promised was recreated. This will be your launching pad, not your losing point. From here on out, you will change the game and steward the storm that's in front of you.

This is your story … own it by believing.

Alissa

Chapter 10: *Pause*

When I was fourteen years old, my momma had the joy of seeing her house being built. I remember watching her sit on the floor, surrounded by color swatches for the walls, carpet options for the floors, and pictures of wood ideas for the kitchen cabinets. For years, she had collected *Better Homes & Gardens* magazines and marked them with tabs so she could put vision to exactly how her perfect house would look. I watched her flip through them often, and I listened to her talk about her plans too many times to count. It wasn't her ultimate dream home being built (she still has a box full of magazines, to this day, for when she builds her dream), but it sure was a joy to practice on.

When the process of piecing that house together began to take place,

I sat back and watched the excitement on her face as she sorted through the details and dreamt about how the completed project would look. When construction began, we would drive by the property often and take pictures of every step it took to make an empty piece of land a home.

You see, it was never a thought of ours to be angry about the wait. We fully understood (from the beginning of planning) that designing a place to hold our family, our memories, and our love would take time and precision. It would have been unrealistic for us to have overnight expectations for something that needed to be built from scratch. So we took joy in watching the plan unfold, and we waited for the work to be completed. Friend, your creating process is going to involve a pause that must be taken, but if you don't understand the need for the "in-between" then you'll rob yourself of the beauty to be found while you wait; I've even learned that it's one of those necessary evils in life that brings forth much wisdom and longevity when it comes to embracing your destiny.

As I look at the story of Noah, I can't help but wonder what his perspective was from inside the ark. For centuries, we've taught his lesson by sharing the truth of what it looks like to remain faithful while building purpose amidst unbelief. We've studied his journey from a one-sided view of how to remain obedient by silencing the voices in our life that say, "God won't do what he said he'll do." But, although Noah's story is one for the books (quite literally in my case), excuse me while I scream, "Plot twist!" because the thing is, his adventure didn't stop when the rain began to fall. In fact, it had just begun. And I think it's time to start acknowledging one of the most untold lessons in the Bible: Why is the pause necessary, and how can I benefit from the wait?

Have you ever tried to picture what it might have been like for Noah? I'd never put much thought into it before, but I imagine that the waves of destruction rang in his ears while they crashed against the sides of the ark. The screams of hopelessness that must have pierced his heart as creation called out from within the storm is difficult for me to wrap my mind around. An aroma of death must have filled the air as well, as life took its last breath and began to float on the surface of what once was. Can you picture it? The sight his eyes must have taken in as he looked out for the first time and processed what it looks like to see promise go through such a terrifying process ... and all that was left to do was float within the pause of it all.

When I began to dig beyond the surface of what we've always been taught of Noah, new questions arose. For instance, do you think he had moments of questioning, or did he realize that *promise* was being carried out during the pause of the storm? What do you think the process of preparation was like for him—spiritually, mentally, and physically—as he learned to embrace destiny?

In case you didn't notice, part 1 of this book was all about putting the pieces back together, learning to build from them, and creating the destiny you want for your life. My ARK ("Acknowledging-Real-Krap") was found through choosing to replace my confession with the truth of who Christ says I am, and using that method allowed me to rebuild and move forward with my life. So what do you do when everything you see, hear, and feel contradicts everything God has promised you? What do you do when you can't escape the destruction taking place around you? I suppose we should do as Noah did, and carry purpose through the flood as we embrace the pause. But if we're not careful, we may allow our pause to place a period on our story. We may allow what was meant to carry us toward promise to instead hold us captive as a prisoner to the storm.

Listen, I know the reality can be more real than the dream at times. I know it may look impossible, and the sound of defeat may seem louder than the voice of destiny. I know the smell of vacancy, hopelessness, pain, and death might be permeating every aspect of your story. I can confidently say I know the truth behind feeling surrounded as well. But I can also say Noah showed us how to be surrounded and still find security in knowing that the pause is not a period.

Sometimes we mistake the silence of waiting as God saying no. But the reality is that the Father is allowing us to catch our breath because where he's taking us requires stamina. Maybe it's time for you to realize that this isn't the end; it's simply a place of breathing. I've found that creation takes place amidst chaos, but you have to be willing to trust the process. Don't put a period on your destiny quite yet! Stop despising your *now*, because it's vital for your *tomorrow*. Understand that you're simply pausing for a breath while waiting for your blessing.

Stop despising your now, because it's vital for your

tomorrow.

The month my divorce was scheduled to be finalized happened to be the same month that would have marked the celebration of our tenth anniversary. It was definitely not the way I'd always imagined we would spend the days leading up to that event, and it wrecked my heart. Ten years should have been such a special milestone. It should have represented a decade of family and love, but it was destroyed by the reality of our life being masked in lies, affairs, and deception. So I begged my lawyer to get me a court date before our anniversary came. I couldn't bear the thought of spending that ten-year-mark legally tied to the man who had walked out on the girls and me. I wanted to save the chance of celebrating such a huge achievement for someone who would love my heart properly.

⋙——▷

One morning while I was cleaning out my closet, I remember finding an old hoody he had given me when we were dating. I was sixteen years old when he gave me that, and it was like I was suddenly thrown back in time as I looked at it sitting in the corner of my closet. All of his stuff had been moved out of the house by that point, so it took me by surprise to see something of his left behind. Although my heart was aching, I was trying desperately to hold on to the promise ahead. I remember putting that hoody on and sitting in the floor of my closet as I wept uncontrollably. Just thinking of how our whole life was falling apart took the breath out of me. Everything was being destroyed, and I didn't know what to do about it or how we had even gotten there in the first place.

My girls were in their playroom making memories, and I was sitting on the other side of the door trying to picture our lives without him in it. I felt a little like Noah that day. I was standing on the edge of purpose, looking out over my life, while watching everything we had known up to that point die in front of me. I could hear the screams of our memories crying out from my heart, and I felt the life we had built for our daughters being destroyed. But even in the flood of my tears, I could hear the still small voice of the Father saying, *Oh, but how much I can change in a year. Do you trust me?*

When tragedy hits your life, it's almost like you're placed on a roller coaster of emotional ups and downs. One minute you're on top of the world and can see the possibility of a new future from a different viewpoint. The next, you're left screaming in anger as you drop from that high to the next low. One day you find yourself in the valley, crying in despair and unable to breathe or move. The next, you're preparing to climb the mountain with a fresh breath of air in your lungs.

I never knew what my day would look like. It was a journey of expecting the unexpected and preparing for a continuous process as I took one step at a time, and I did that by becoming a voice for myself in the valley. I knew faith had to become the substance that brought me toward the evidence of promise as I overcame that trial in my life. But in order to see it, I had to speak it.

Let me pull back the curtain to one of the biggest pieces of advice you'll ever be given during the dark times of your life, guys. *You,* dear heart, are your greatest prophet! *You* are your biggest advocate or your worst enemy. The things you speak over yourself will become what you believe about yourself, and those beliefs will determine the outcome of your situation.

You, dear heart, are your greatest prophet!

During that season of my life, I had family encouraging me and friends doing the best they could to uplift me, but the problem was that no one understood exactly what I was dealing with because they weren't me. I felt alone because no one was walking in my shoes, and no one was knocking down my door to give me a *"right now"* word from the Lord that would get me out of the hell I was walking through.

I had a handful of promises spoken over my life by men and women of God along the way, but those prophecies and people weren't what got me through the darkness in my life. You know what got me through? Me. I was the answer to the destiny in my life! I was my biggest voice of victory! I was the most listened to and most *heard* prophet in my life.

Confession #10: Voice memo became the voice of promise during the pause in my life.

One day, through anger and emotional exhaustion, I decided that no one could help me. I was pressure washing my house in the heat of the summer while listening to Pandora Radio. Beyoncé's song "Me, Myself, and I" came on, and I thought to myself, "Yes! She's so right. … All I have in the end is myself. No one else understands where I'm at, how I need them to pray, or what kind of advice to give me. I have to learn to rely on myself if I want a different life than what I have." And from that moment forward, I began to take advantage of the mountains by recording a voice memo. That's what changed the game during that season of my life, and I firmly believe—with every fiber of my being—that it could help you change yours.

I've always had a writer's heart, but this was different for me. Instead of taking my heart to empty pages with pen and paper, I learned to press record and fill the voice memos on my iPhone with prayers, songs, and declarations for my life (I share these with you in the back of the book). Pressing record became a way of living for me during the summer of 2017. Anytime I felt that I could see even the slightest glimmer of hope at the end of the dark, dirt road ahead of me, I would hit record by taking advantage of the mountaintop I was on.

Some days it was as simple as speaking the truth about who the Word says I am; I did that by reading scriptures over myself that helped combat the lies I believed. Some days it was a full-on prayer session while

I went to war in the spirit and waited for the storm to pass; I did that by interceding for my kids, my ministry, my future, my dreams, and my heart. Other days consisted of my guitar and me in the quiet of the night, working through songs of healing by putting melodies to my pain with praise. But no matter how it came about, I made it a habit to consistently hit record so I could encourage myself during the pause of life.

I often thought to myself how silly I was for doing that. I mean, who records themself talking to, well ... themself? And it may have been unusual in the beginning, but it all began to make sense during the moments of despair. When it felt like there was no breath left within my lungs and I was all alone, I learned to push play. When I couldn't bear to lift my head off my pillow and found no willpower to open my eyes, I pushed play. When the night's silence screamed out to me with lies—telling me I'd never survive that season of my life—I would **PUSH PLAY**! Pushing play allowed my ears the opportunity to hear *my own voice* speak truth about my circumstance. There's something so powerful about that process! I became my own voice of victory, encouragement, and life in the moments where I had no willpower to keep on going. That's how I learned that I don't need anyone to knock down my door with a word from the Lord in order for me to get back up; all I need to do is push play and listen to the biggest prophet in my life—**ME**.

Turns out, the voice that ended up saving my life was my own.

Turns out, the voice that ended up saving my life

was my own.

Have you ever been on a roller coaster ride? Have you ever experienced the excitement of climbing to the top of the first big mountain? Do you remember taking in the sites of your surroundings as you waited with anticipation for the first big drop to take place? That's where you push record, friend! That's where you take advantage of the pause. That's where you fill your memos with words that speak *promise*. And it's in that moment—the in-between—that you allow creation to take place! It's vital that you preserve those moments and become aware of those opportunities because you can never get them back.

That simple action of recording the moment began to heal my heart in more ways than I ever imagined. It brought substance to my faith on days where I found myself in the valley, and it allowed hope to take root in my heart once more. I couldn't always control the emotional ups and downs of my healing heart, but I could breathe during the pause knowing that *promise* was on its way. Guys, hitting record during moments where I felt I could catch my breath gave me the opportunity to push play when I couldn't breathe at all. It allowed me to surround myself with an atmosphere of my own voice speaking the truth about what the Word of God says I can have and who the Father says I am. It created an opportunity for me to become the prophet over my life, and it began to reshape my belief about my situation, even when I couldn't see it at all.

So hear me today. If you feel a little like Noah right now, please know that it's in the pause that you must push play on what God has said about you! Everything you see around you might look like death, but that's where creation takes place. You have not been forgotten on the ark. You've been placed in position to be protected, and you've been marked with God's rainbow of promise for your future.

It's in the pause that you must push play on what God has said about you!

Push record … breathe … and press play to listen. This will change everything. #AskMeHowIKnow

Confession

Voice memo became the voice of promise during the pause in my life.

Truth

You are the biggest prophet in your life. Press record and push play.

Journal entry
August 31, 2017

Hello,

I'm sitting here going through my calendar and watching Kins do her homeschool work. And I've suddenly realized that we only have four months left to the year. ... Four months.

I immediately thought, So much for this year being a year of completion. So much for my dreams coming true. With four months left there isn't enough time to see anything powerful take place, or any projects for ministry happen.

But right as that thought crossed my mind, I heard the Holy Spirit ask me, *How many months did it take for your entire life to fall apart?*

I quickly checked the calendar and did the math—two months fighting for my marriage and two months finalizing our divorce. So the answer is four. It only took four months for a lifetime to crumble into a thousand pieces.

That's when a light bulb clicked inside me as I heard the Father say, I can redeem the time stolen. Four months gone, and four months gained. Doors of opportunity, completion, and restoration are coming to your life. How will you steward this thing? Do you trust *me?*

I didn't write about it yet (I don't know why) ... but the divorce is final and officially over. I thought I'd be a mess when I received the call from my lawyer about the court date, but the truth is, I didn't feel a thing. I was numb when I heard her voice on the other end of the line, "Alissa, we did it! We're getting you this divorce three days before your tenth anniversary takes place. See you at court at 9 a.m., and bring you a witness." At that moment, I sat down and began to play the songs I wrote throughout this nightmare. My sister was there, and I needed to feel something more than the numbing truth that this was over. ... So I sang to her.

When divorce day arrived, I took my daddy to court with me. He has walked with me through the hell of this entire process and kept me from burning up. There were so many nights where I was scared to be alone at the house with my kids, and it was my daddy who came and slept on the couch to keep us safe. When I needed someone to cry, scream, cuss, and vent to, he was the one who listened. When I couldn't see any hope for my future, he encouraged me to stand in faith. My daddy spoke truth over me—without suffocating me with Scripture—while allowing me to walk out my process. In doing so, he watched me heal over time ... and he healed with me. So I couldn't think of anyone I wanted by my side more than him when my divorce day finally approached.

My ex-husband wasn't there. There was no need. It was a non-contested case, and all I wanted (more than anything) was to get it over with. My lawyer began to state my case to the judge, and everything fell into slow motion. An entire life of memories flashed before my eyes—date nights, our wedding, college life, recording music, having babies, doing ministry—it all surged in like a flood. But then the memories screeched to a halt when the judge asked me if I wanted to change my name back to my maiden name—to which I said yes.

After all was said and done, the judge sealed the moment with the crash of his gavel, and I felt numbness shatter around me as the waves of emotion began to rush in.

For weeks, I had prayed while preparing a final goodbye letter to the man I called "husband" for nearly a decade. It was full of one thank-you after another as I listed out everything I was grateful to him for:

Thank you for our girls. They're holding me down and

loving my heart back to health. Thank you for teaching me how

valuable a whole and complete family is ... I'll never take it for

granted again.

Thank you for pushing me out of my comfort zone

because, without you leaving, I never would have found out

how strong I truly am.

Thank you for showing me that I don't need anyone else in order to pursue my dreams—I am enough on my own.

Thank you for breaking me, because now I'm able to put the pieces back together differently.

Thank you for giving me the opportunity to conquer my fears; I've learned to look them straight in the face and laugh without fear of the future.

Thank you for not seeing me. I've learned to see myself, and now I know just how beautiful I truly am.

Thank you for showing me what love isn't, because it'll remind me to steward love with grace and to always remember that love is not an emotion—it's an everyday choice.

Thank you for these ten years. I've learned a lot, grown a lot, and emerged into a woman I never thought I could be. I truly couldn't have done it without you. It hurts to let go, but I know there's a man out there who will treat me like his treasure and not his trash.

I ended it with this and meant it with all my heart:

Goodbye to my husband. I love you, I forgive you, and I wish you the best in life. Be better and strive hard for the good things in life. Open up to people and let down your wall. Allow God to be real in your life and seek the company of those who will help you be the best version of you. Use your talents for God, and he will bless them.

But more than anything, show our kids what love is by being the first man to love them and not break their heart. They're the most important things in your life. Do good by them. Show them God in your leadership and love toward them. Please remember that what you are to them is what they'll look for in a man when they grow up and fall in love.

There is happiness out there for you ... now go find it.

Here's to nearly ten years and not counting. You have loved me, and you have broken me. But I will rise from the ashes as a new woman. I will be better for it; I already am. And I will never be the same again.

All my love,

Alissa

As soon as I arrived back in town from the courthouse, I took my letter (and the hoody he'd given me all those years ago) and left it behind his screen door, sealed with a kiss. I promised myself that from that moment forward, I'd be a new woman, and the future was mine to own.

P.M.

Before I go to sleep, I want to record a funny thing that happened today. After feeling in my spirit that I'll have four months gained after the four months lost, Brandon Holt messaged me on Facebook.

He let me know that he's sorry to hear about the divorce, and he said he's praying for the girls and me. He said to let him know if I need anything and mentioned that he wants to hear my music. I don't know why, but I feel like this is the beginning of something amazing. I have no doubt that God is in this thing and working in my favor.

I am going to keep moving forward.

Alissa

Chapter 11: *The Middle Seat*

If you've never been on an airplane before, let me go ahead and let you in on a little secret. Your seat matters!

Without fail, the first question I ask my bae every time we head to the airport is, "What seat do I have on this flight? Please tell me it's not the middle seat." It pains me to say this, but it's your girl (me) who ends up inheriting this dreaded seat most of the time. And if you've ever been on a plane—or the victim of the middle seat somewhere—then you know exactly what I'm talking about and why this is the seat that must be filled even though nobody wants it.

This special seat leaves you squished in between two strangers and feeling like it's your responsibility to become as small as you possibly can so you won't invade their personal space (even though you have none of your own). When you're assigned the middle seat, you're left to secretly intercede for the well-being of your nostrils, *Please God, don't let me get stuck in between two people with horrible body odor, unforgivably bad breath, or gassy stomachs*—because secretly rubbing travel size perfume on your wrists and smelling it the whole flight is not fun (ask me how I know). This dreaded seat will have you walking down the aisle of the plane like an undercover spy, secretly scanning every person around your row to see if they look like "talkers." You'll be double-checking your ticket to see how long it'll take for you to get out of that cramped space and back into open, fresh air.

My point? No one likes the middle seat. Especially me.

On our way to the airport this morning my husband turned to me and said, "Babe, don't even ask if you'll be getting the middle seat. The answer is yes."

Immediately, I was dreading the entire trip. And my face made sure to notify Bran of my feelings. Here's the truth, the middle seat makes me uncomfortable, and unless my husband wants a cuddle partner the entire flight (like he has a choice, right?), I'll be thinking "skinny" the whole way there so I don't disturb the people beside me. But with some banter back and forth, he playfully said, "You know what? Write a book about it! Call it *The Middle Seat.* Find some wisdom in how you can make this more enjoyable."

Well, it may not be an entire book, but here you go, Bran! A chapter completely dedicated to you and your inspiration!

So I had been rewarded the middle seat, bae willingly accepted the aisle seat beside me, and with all the interceding I'd done from then till now, I honestly had high hopes for the person sitting on the other side of me. But what happened next was glorious. Ladies and Gents, I am pleased to tell you that the window seat person never showed up! Do you know what that means? The middle seat is empty because I upgraded to the window seat—where I'm currently sitting as I write this chapter. I repeat, the middle seat is empty, and we have more room to ourselves!

Let me tell you, basking in this glorious window-seat view and enjoying my extra space has shown me how this can represent the seat of promise in your life. It holds a view that no one else gets to see, which allows you to enjoy the journey from a different perspective than the other passengers around you. With a new outlook on life, you're given the opportunity to look outside of your current situation and find beauty.

The aisle seat is quite the opposite. It can represent the seat of pain in your life. I'm reminded of this because I just saw the flight attendant crash her snack cart into my husband's knee and then shove him over as she continued down the aisle. This seat has a view that consists of nothing more than what's directly in front of you. It leaves you looking over your shoulder to make sure no one else hurts you as they pass by.

And the middle seat can represent the in-between stage of your journey. It's a place where you aren't necessarily guarding yourself from pain, but you adopt the mindset that it's your job to become as small as possible so you don't disrupt your seat neighbors. It comes with a partial view of both pain and promise and leaves you to focus on the dear soul sitting directly in front of you.

How many times do we find ourselves in between pain and promise? Have you been there? Are you there right now? I've come to recognize that my focus in that position zeroes in on three main things.

1. The pain I don't want to feel anymore.
2. The promise I can't seem to grab ahold of.
3. All the people who seem to be ahead of me.

All three seats are on the same journey, the same flight, and are headed toward the same destination—yet we fix our attention on the *seat,* rather than on the *direction* we're headed. Friend, if you aren't careful, and get so caught up on the position of your seat, you'll forget that the posture of the plane is taking us all to the same place. Sometimes you need to change your perspective in order to embrace purpose. We all have destiny waiting for us to arrive. The question is, what seat will you live in?

Sometimes you need to change your perspective in order to embrace purpose.

After I began to walk through the process of healing, I slowly began embracing the middle seat. It was there that I began to see a glimpse of the window view's promise, but at the same time, I could also see how painful the aisle seat can really be. For so long, I allowed myself to live in the aisle seat of pain by making a bed out of my circumstances and lying down in them. I can admit now that I allowed myself to exist there for far too long.

If you could see me right now, you'd see my current situation of a comfortable seat and a view I wasn't meant to have. My ticket states that the middle seat is mine, and the seating arrangement in the airline's computer system confirms it. Because of this, I could have easily accepted the assignment by staying put until I reach my destination. And unfortunately, this is a common thing many of us can relate to in different areas of our life. When an assignment comes to label us with grief, shame, worthlessness, and—for lack of better words—*filters*, most of us would sit in bitterness about our position by becoming angry at people who are sitting in promise while we're holding on to our dirt.

Too many times, we don't understand that we have the power to MOVE OVER, but that's exactly what I did today. When I realized that no one showed up to claim promise (the window seat), I took the liberty to move over and leave the middle seat empty—and you should too! You are the only one who can claim promise for your life. Your ticket may say to take a seat in divorce, loss, tragedy, abuse, and failure, but there's a seat of promise waiting to be claimed. Stop being comfortable with being uncomfortable! Stop settling for a glimpse of the promise by maintaining a seat of pain. Move over and leave the middle seat empty! You'll be much happier over here.

Confession #11: I used to think seats were assigned instead of

chosen.

As I look at the empty seat next to me, I'm reminded of the process I've taken during my life. With every seat came a shift in my mindset. Those shifts made me more and more aware of the fact that life is what I choose for it to be, and that a solution can be found behind every circumstance. Over the last two years, I've found a better understanding of the fact that my seat was never *assigned* to me; I've always had the choice of where to sit during my journey.

A woman just reached out to me—as Bran and I sit in the Dallas airport waiting for our next flight—with a story of broken dreams and painful circumstances. Some of her message read, "I'm devastated, hurt, and broken. I feel like all my dreams are dead, while I watch others live their dreams out. I don't know what I've done to make God so angry. I've done everything I know to do, but I feel like God has forgotten me." While I read that, I immediately thought to myself that this young lady has already assigned herself a seat labeled "dead dreams." If she isn't careful, she'll shift from the aisle seat to the middle seat, but she'll never fully sit in promise unless she makes a choice to move over.

Listen to me. The seat you choose determines what you see, and what you see determines what you believe you can have. Choosing to sit in pain positions you to see only what's directly ahead—all the pain, hurt, tragedy, inconvenience, frustration, and fear. Pain will shape a belief system that says you'll never heal and always hurt. Choosing to sit in the middle seat positions you to believe that pain is always at your side and promise is always up ahead. That'll make you think you're stuck in between the two forever, and you'll be left feeling hopeless and defeated.

These are false truths!

The seat you choose determines what you see, and what you see determines what you believe you can have.

What is it that God says you can have? What does his Word say is true?

When God gave me the promise of "four months," I found myself glued to the middle seat. Although I was no longer in a place of constant torment, I was still sitting beside pain while only catching a glimpse of promise up ahead. And it took months of me shifting from seat to seat on an emotional roller coaster to realize I could claim my seat of promise while waiting for the plane to arrive.

So many times, we're waiting to "arrive" before we can be assigned to our destiny. Arriving, for you, may look something like healing, financial stability, closure, joy, finishing that book you wanted to write, starting a family, moving on from that painful relationship, or stepping out into that business endeavor. Once you feel like you've finally set your foot on the timeline of that reality, *then* you can say your assignment is finally here. Now that your hands can touch that business idea, your assignment has begun. Now that you're healthy and no longer struggling with sickness or being out of shape, your future can begin. Now that you've finally written that book, you can press start on the assignment for your life.

No! God wants to assign your seat to you long before you ever arrive at your destination, but here's the catch: *You* get to choose where you sit. How would that change the way you steward your *now* while you wait for your promise? God's desire is always to assign you a seat in promise, but his grace allows us to choose what seat we want to sit in.

His grace allows us to choose what seat we

want to sit in.

»»——▷

Do you remember those voice memos I recorded during the worst times of my life? That was me stewarding my *now* by choosing to sit in the seat of promise while I waited to arrive. I remember the moment I found my ex's hoody in the closet. I remember the reality of pain, loss, rejection, and abandonment. Nothing was more real to me than the feelings I was dealing with in that moment. But do you know what I did next?

Once I peeled myself up off the floor, I made my way to the guest room where my ex-husband's things had been packed in boxes a month before. That's where I made the decision to get out of the aisle seat and shift to promise. That's where I chose to leave the middle seat empty. With tears flowing down my face, and my girls' voices in the background playing with dolls, I got my phone out and pressed record. That was the moment I created with my pieces while prophesying over my pain, long before I saw the evidence of promise. Even while wearing a hoody that brought hurt, I held on to promise and spoke the truth behind the Word of God. I chose to make myself look out the window of hope and visualize what my promise would look like. I prayed in faith for my future, my family, my ministry, and my God-ordained husband. That moment of feeling allowed me to place hope in the ground as I waited for the evidence of my faith to show up.

Moving from the middle seat to the window seat was significant for me, but before I could see a clear view of promise I had to learn to become more like Peter. And if you immediately thought about Peter the disciple, let me redirect you toward a different Peter ... the one who defeated Captain Hook and befriended Tinkerbell. That's right, I'm talking about Peter Pan. He was a childhood favorite of mine, but just in case you didn't grow up knowing who the lost boys were, let me fill you in on some details. There's a famous scene where Tinkerbell coaches Peter so he can learn to fly. There were two requirements that had to be met, and I'm here to tell you that these are requirements *you* must meet as well. So let's review…

The first thing you must do in order to fly is "find your happy thought." Friend, how can you expect to get up off the ground and rise above what's keeping you shackled to pain, defeat, and yesterday if you're constantly filling your mind with, well … pain, defeat, and yesterday? It's time to find your happy thoughts by changing your thought life and what it is you're meditating on!

The second thing is simple, "You must *believe*!" Without the belief that you can rise above your current situation, your feet will never leave the ground you've chained yourself to. Listen, you cannot expect flight in your life when you've fallen captive to fear and complacency. Your faith (or in this case, belief) will set out to do whatever your mind says you can do. If you believe the truth of God's Word and what he says he is, then you can have it! If you believe what your current situation is saying about you, then you will have it!

Listen, you cannot expect flight in your life when you've fallen captive to fear and complacency.

For me, everything changed when I pressed record on a prayer that determined what seat I'd sit in as I positioned myself toward destiny. That recording became evidence of what it sounds like to hear faith take flight. With every push of that play button, I found proof that feelings can be planted with hope, and faith can grow into the evidence of what Christ can do. It all started with me sitting in the aisle seat of pain in my closet floor, and it allowed me the opportunity to move toward the seat of promise by refusing to get stuck in the middle. I simply made the decision to move over, and you can too.

But that doesn't mean the decision will be easy. In fact, on days where I felt myself grabbing hold of the middle seat again, I'd push play on my Hebrews 11:1 prayer. That voice memo, dated August 7, 2017, reminded me of the day I made a choice to claim something I couldn't necessarily see, and it continues to prove to me just how faithful God is when you look out the window of promise and declare what is to come. Do you know what that did for me?

That voice memo, from the day I chose to press record and move over, became my marriage vows on April 27, 2018. As we stood at the altar in front of our family and friends, I surprised Brandon with a clip of me praying for my future husband. He could hear the feelings of pain but also feel the faith of promise within my voice. That prayer became tangible evidence for me to grab hold of as I stood looking in the eyes of the man I'd imagined from a window view and said, "I do."

See? Your seat matters! So what if your ticket says divorced, abused, forgotten, or failure. Move over! Get out of your own way and make a choice to claim your seat of promise! God assigned you that spot long ago.

> But those who wait for the Lord [who expect,
>
> > look for, and hope in Him]
>
> Will gain new strength and renew their power;
>
> They will lift up their wings [and rise up
>
> > close to God] like eagles [rising toward the sun];
>
> They will run and not become weary,
>
> They will walk and not grow tired. (Isaiah 40:31, AMP)

Notice that this scripture says you'll wear strength when you wait, and you'll fly before you run or walk. That tells me that your foot doesn't have to touch the ground for you to walk in destiny. Take advantage of the flight and learn to soar in faith. That's where you become closer to God and gain understanding of who you are. Stop waiting for the perfect condition, complete restoration, closure, or a future version of yourself. Realize that you can choose your assignment NOW.

Confession

I used to think seats were assigned instead of chosen.

Truth

Your seat matters! God assigned you a seat of purpose long before you arrived at your destination!

Journal entry
October 7, 2017

Hello,

Tonight was magical. Something happened when I least expected it, and I feel a shift in my heart. It might sound crazy, but a spark that hasn't been there in a very long time has been reignited; my face has found a smile where a frown had made a home. I'm in awe of how faithful the Father is.

To be truthful, I've spent the last couple of months untying knots I'd created. I haven't written in this journal for a while because I've been avoiding areas I needed to address. It's easier for me to not write when I want to ignore something. So that's exactly what I did.

Loneliness is not fun, and if you're not careful, it'll leave you trading love for companionship. Emotional ties are easy to fall into when you don't like to be alone. And man, oh man, I've unfortunately found that to be true over this season of my life. It's easy to numb lonely nights with long-distance phone calls and gain confidence by being affirmed by the opposite sex. Old friendships can quickly grow into something more when you're comfortable—even when it's not the right thing for your life.

These past two months have been a process of character testing for me. I've failed in some areas and passed in others. This journey hasn't been an easy road, but I've continued to walk down it nevertheless. Thank God for the Holy Spirit and his gentle correction and careful nudging. I don't know where I would be without it.

After I course-corrected and reminded myself of the promise in my life (to live life led by the Holy Spirit), I had the least expected thing happen. I was sitting in my living room last night, with my sister and her fiancé, when my phone lit up with a notification; Brandon Holt was doing a livestream on Facebook. I've been following him and his ministry for two years on social media. We've never really interacted, other than following each other's music and ministry and saying an occasional "Hey!" when we catch each other's livestreams. The first time we ever really messaged each other was when he reached out to say how sorry he was to hear about my divorce.

Well, I decided to jump in on his worship session, and he saw my name pop up on his screen when I clicked the notification to watch him. He was sick with a sinus infection and was doing a "pass the mic night" where he'd invite people on to sing for his followers, and almost immediately after I logged on, he asked if I would join his stream to sing for him. He playfully said, "Forget this, I'm inviting you. If you don't answer my invite, then we can't be friends anymore!"

I was freaking out because I'd just got done exercising and looked like a train wreck. My heart felt like it was literally beating out of my chest as I sat there in my workout clothes—barely any makeup on and un-tamed hair. And I'm not sure why, but for some reason my finger pressed the green accept button before my brain could process what was going on. BOOM! There I was. Live on his Facebook feed with no way of turning back.

When I saw Brandon's face looking at me from the other side of that screen, something happened. There was a shift in my heart. And all of a sudden, I didn't care about the other 200+ people who were watching us. I immediately felt things I'd never felt toward him before. He asked what I was going to sing, and the only song I could think of was "Good Good Father." It had been one of my anthems throughout that season, but it was also a popular song that B often sang on his feed.

Something overcame me, and I sang my little heart out for all those people on his broadcast. I didn't care about how I looked anymore. I just stopped what I was doing and began to do what I do best—worship. He was blown away. And I couldn't stop smiling at him, because some kind of connection took place in that moment that I don't have words for. The only thing I can say is that there's a shifting taking place.

Everyone online seemed to really enjoy it, too, when B decided to throw his Elsa-themed tissue box at the camera and say, "That girl just *sang*! She's just oily!"

Later on that night, he posted on Instagram about me; he shared a screenshot of me singing on the broadcast while his hands were raised in the air. Both of us were smiling all goofy, and he let everyone know to follow me. He also said he wants to write me soon—which he did immediately after. He private-messaged me, we had some small chitchat back and forth, and I gave him my number to connect with him. But, honestly, I didn't know if I should expect a call anytime soon.

I wasn't expecting anything, but we connected like we'd known each other all our life. I kept thinking, Um, this is THE Brandon Holt. How are we connecting so well? I've followed him for years, and we've had small talk back and forth, but this is different.

Well, today he called me for the first time, only one day after I gave him my number. We talked all through the day as he traveled, and then he called me tonight, around 10 p.m., after he finished a worship consult. He started off by saying, "I'm a questions guy. I just want to get to know you. I hope that's ok."

We laid everything on the table and talked about divorce, kids, bad relationships, where our hearts are at, what our dreams are, our likes and dislikes, greatest weaknesses, greatest strengths, pet peeves, favorite foods, movies, holidays, dream vacation spots ... *all* the things. I kind of wondered to myself if he was trying to feel me out and see if I was interested, but then I thought, *Nah, this is THE Brandon Holt. ... I'm just Alissa.*

It was 5:30 a.m. when we got off the phone, and he ended the call by saying, "Where have you been the last twelve years? I think I might just make you my wife!"

I laughed as I remembered a journal entry of mine from around my birthday; I'd had a dream that I was having dinner with a man I knew would be my husband. The statements Brandon made during our conversation were the same statements made in my dream. I read him the journal entry, and we sat there completely shocked by it all. Is it crazy to say I feel deep down in my heart that I just met my husband tonight? This is crazy, right?

I went to bed feeling like I'm living a fairy tale. Did I just meet the man I've been praying for? I know this all sounds insane, but I just feel it in my bones.

It's peace. Home. A knowing.

I don't know how this will play out, but I'm ready to see where it leads.

Alissa

Chapter 12: *Unfiltered*

In just two short days, I'll enter a new decade and embrace my thirties with arms open wide. It still amazes me to see all the healing, restoration, and fulfillment the Father has walked me through. About this time two years ago, I was downing a bottle of wine and praying to God that I could make it through my birthday sane. This year, I'm writing the final chapters of a book that tells of how God is always faithful to keep his promises, even when we can't see it. This process hasn't been easy to walk through, and it also hasn't been easy for many people to accept.

Not long after Brandon and I made our relationship public to our social media following, I was surprised to find people who were mad about the restoration in my life.

I'll never forget the day I posted a picture of me smiling from ear to ear. I'd asked my sister to take some shots of the girls and me so we could have a way to look back at where God has brought us from. One of the pictures she captured showed nothing but pure joy as I was right in the middle of a belly laugh. When I saw the photos, I couldn't help but think to myself, *There she is. Oh, how I've missed her.* I took the liberty of using that photo to encourage people in their walk toward finding their smile because I know the journey far too well. My post read:

> Finding my smile and learning to love it was a huge journey for me. Misery can become a good friend; you can end up purposely making yourself miserable out of comfort. That is where I found myself for too many years, and happiness was uncharted territory for me. I remember the day I found my smile again. I told God, "How crazy is this that I'm having to teach my face how to smile again?" Literally, my mouth had a permanent frown.
>
> I want to encourage someone to learn to smile and rest in the joy of the Lord. It's not easy. It's a process. It's tough. But if you take one step at a time, to focus on your ministry in declaring who Jesus is over your life (rather than declaring your misery), you'll find your joy once more.

Almost immediately after I posted that, I received a comment from a follower saying, "Must be nice to have joy and see God restore you. Try going seven years without God showing up for you. You don't know pain. … It wasn't even a full year before you found someone to make you happy. Cute smile though."

And the same thing happened when my husband and I decided to share our struggle with infertility. (I'll talk more about that in the next chapter.) After I had surgery to increase our chances for conceiving baby Holt, we posted a picture to tell everyone I was in recovery, and we asked them to continue praying for our journey. Our hope was to gain the prayers of those who were willing to stand in faith with us and to partner with others who can relate by letting them know they're not alone. But not long after the post went public, I received a comment from a follower saying, "Ha! Try praying for seven years with your husband, only to have a pastor's wife say that God's withholding from me because I'm not clean enough in my soul. At least you have TWO children. I'm childless."

When I read those comments, I was overwhelmed with sadness for the people who posted them. I wasn't angry at them for speaking their truth. I was simply filled with compassion for their lives because I recognized the spirit of hurt behind the words on the screen. One woman didn't understand that my smile was found through a Savior who'd healed my heart. Instead, she contributed my joy to the man who'd walked into my life. The other woman didn't understand how I could possibly want more children when I already have two of my own. Instead of showing compassion for my husband who has no children of *his own* yet, she used words that cut and revealed the pain behind her own journey. Both circumstances showed the process behind finding and fighting for promise. And it taught me that no matter what side you're standing on, people will always find ways to be mad at you for embracing your dirt.

People will always find ways to be mad at you for

embracing your dirt.

Listen to me, it's easy to judge the fulfillment of someone's promise from the outside, but you may not know of all the days and nights where someone walked through hell to get to where they are now.

The first lady had no idea that I'd fought the beauty behind my smile since I was fourteen years old. She had no idea that being raped by someone whom I thought loved me had stolen my love for myself. She had no clue that I'd abused my body for nearly eleven years with eating disorders and self-hate. She wasn't with me for nearly a decade as I fought for my marriage and lived a filtered life of "freedom." There was no way to recognize from the outside that I'd fought a battle within myself for more than half of my life that screamed, "I hate myself!" The restoration of joy didn't come from a person—it came from a Father who had taken me down a long and dirty journey toward embracing my destiny.

The second lady saw our family and assumed it was full and complete. She filtered her story of infertility through the lens of what it looks like to be childless, but she didn't take into consideration that my husband feels the truth behind her pain. Instead, she saw two beautiful girls—rather than our pain of one negative test after another for over a year. With photos of smiling faces and children by our side on social media, she didn't experience the moment we were told that our chances of having a child *together* were slim. She wasn't in the room with us before my surgery when we prayed for a better chance of conceiving, but she did show up on our social media post afterward with words of pain and destruction.

The restoration, healing, and promise in my life were expensive, and they cost me more things than I can count. I lost relationships with family members who became jealous of God's faithfulness in my life. I had friends walk out on me because I was only beneficial to them when I was broken. I lost my identity and had to build a brand-new life from scratch. Everything about my life changed, and I fought like hell to make sure change didn't end up chaining me to my pain.

I can honestly say I still scratch my head from time to time and ask, *God, why me? Why did you fulfill your Word so quickly in my life? How am I any different from the rest?* The truth is, I'm not exactly sure of the answer. I wish I could tell you a secret formula and give you a detailed list of to-dos for you to see your life fall back into place. But all I can say is that from the moment I began to walk this journey out, I made the choice to not allow my dirt to define me.

On the flip side, though, I've found that the fear to fight for promise can put you in a position of bitterness toward those who are willing to fight despite the fear. I know that because I've been there. I've done it. I've sat back and watched others fight faithfully for what the Word says they can have, and I've done it with my nose held high, allowing sharp words of judgment toward them to slide off my tongue. And to tell you the truth, it wasn't necessarily because I didn't want to see promise fulfilled in their life. No, it boiled down to the harsh reality that their fight made me look weak. Their fight showed me what I, too, was capable of doing, and it made me confront the fact that my dirt had become a pillow for my head while theirs had become purpose in their hand. … I hated it. I hated seeing other people fight for promise while I sat in complacency—and that was the same hate I began to see others show toward my husband and me when we began to fight for our destiny.

Friend, the cycle of defeat had followed me around for too many years to count, and somewhere along the way, I got tired of letting it win. I wish I could say I maintained a faith-filled life by keeping my head lifted high during that process. But as you know by reading this book, that wasn't always the case. Perfection wasn't the story behind my journey. The process within my pages shows that I was continually being postured toward promise, even when I fell short.

If I tried to sell you an act of being holier-than-thou in order to claim destiny for my life, then I'd be lying. My journey showed moments of defeat where painful nights were numbed with pills or alcohol. My pages confess outbursts of anger where I'd cuss, scream, and break things to release my rage. I had days where depression kept me in bed and kept me from eating or taking a shower. I fought deeply rooted blame, unforgiveness, and hatred toward others and myself and used wrong companionship to ease the hurt of feeling alone and unlovable.

Do y'all want the unfiltered truth about my process?

Confession #12: I did *all* the things religion told me not to do, but I still saw promise fulfilled in my life.

How is that possible? What made me different? How come God didn't punish me for not being perfect on my journey? How come good behavior isn't the requirement for promise to be kept? Those are all questions I asked myself (a countless number of times) along the way. And the only real answer I can give you is that I consistently did one thing without fail. Are you ready?

I repositioned my posture toward promise every time I fell out of alignment with his Word. In other words, friends, I repented.

I've heard the word *repent* so many times within the church walls. It was defined by "saying you're sorry." It's displayed at full altar calls with wet cheeks as people encounter an emotional experience with the word "Sorry" rather than with the person "Savior." Hear me out, though, guys. I'm not saying that all altar calls aren't a genuine experience, or that true change doesn't take place in the hearts of people when they answer those invitations (because it does). What I am saying is that I've personally experienced—and even seen in countless other lives around me—how the altar brought tear-stained shirts and true conviction but the stronghold of bondage remained once I walked back out of the church doors. So listen, being sorry doesn't keep you consistent in your lifestyle; having a Savior does.

Being sorry doesn't keep you consistent in your lifestyle;

having a Savior does.

The old saying remains true: actions speak louder than words. When it boils down to it, repentance isn't found in saying sorry; it's found when you experience the Savior for who he truly is.

It wasn't until I understood that God isn't angry at me—but accepts me just as I am—that my mind was placed in a position to change its thinking about my situation. My actions began to line up with what the *Word* had for me more than with what *I* wanted. When I placed myself in a position of grace (by being repentant), it gave me the willpower to keep going. What did that look like exactly? It looked like me recognizing that the nature of who I am is wrapped up in *flesh*, and it took grace to help me stay accountable to my actions and behavior. Requiring of myself a list of rules, regulations, and religious checkmarks was not the answer to restoration in my life. The fulfillment behind his Word came when I stopped denying the fact that I'm flesh and blood and allowed my spirit-man the ability to course-correct my posture when I got off track.

I began healing when I stopped shaming myself for feeling. Realizing that I'm created to be an emotional being is what changed my understanding of how the Father sees me. I found myself in a place of learning as I walked in the spirit (the influence of Christ) and gave my flesh (human nature) grace to catch up. It was then that I realized the truth behind restoration and healing—it's a *process of promise,* not a position or place.

I don't know why restoration worked for me so fast, but maybe it isn't working for you because you have more faith in the religion of saying sorry than you do in the relationship of a Savior. I know it may shock you to read this, but Jesus is not mad at you for sinning. In fact, the dirt from your sin won't even send you to hell. Your fault doesn't come from doing what humanity does—it comes from denying him the opportunity to take you by the hand and do life with you.

I can already hear some of you now as you read that. "What? How could she say this? What nerve she has to give people permission to embrace the dirt from their sin!" Here's the thing. I'm not giving you permission to embrace your dirt. I'm giving you permission to embrace your destiny by understanding that your dirt does not determine your ability to be everything God has created you to be, and your sin does not disqualify you from doing everything God has called you to do.

For God so loved the world that he gave his one and only Son,

that whoever believes in him shall not perish but have eternal life.

(John 3:16)

For most of my life, I believed sin would keep me from Heaven and more checkmarks on my religious rulebook would bring me closer to the

Father's heart. But the Word clearly states that the only requirement for relationship with Christ is to *believe* in him. Nowhere under the new-covenant law does it say our sin is what keeps us out of Heaven. In fact, it's our *unbelief* that keeps us from inheriting the promised life he has for us. So it's time for the lie that says, "sin is what separates us from the love of Christ," to be unfiltered. To be frank, I'd say it's time for this lie to just go ahead and die.

Understand this, our ability to truly know the Father requires us to allow him to truly know us. We have to be willing to unfilter the truth behind our life and trust that he's a loving God who has a plan to bring us hope and a future (see Jeremiah 29:11).

Our ability to truly know the Father requires us to allow him to truly know us.

My daughter Kinsleigh (who just had her 9th birthday) has entered a new phase of life over the past year. One of the things I've taught my girls, from the beginning stages of their lives, is that love does two things: it listens, and it learns. Through this, I've established a relationship with them that proves I'll listen when they need to talk their feelings out, but that I'll also give them opportunity to learn in those moments.

One day Kins came to me whispering, "strawberry kisses," in my ear. When they were much younger, those words were code for "secret time";

I'd respond with, "I promise." She then took me by the hand and led me to her room. I sat down on her bed as she shut the door behind her and locked it. I knew then that this must be serious, because she made sure no one could come in. Then she started the conversation by putting her finger over her mouth and whispering, "Shh ... this is just for you only. I need to talk to you, Mommy ... but I'm scared that you'll be angry at me."

Instantly, I reassured her of my love by saying, "Baby, I'm here to sit and listen to everything you have to say, and then we'll talk it out. You don't have to be scared of anything."

With big ol' tears welling up in her eyes, she began to pour her secrets out to me, one by one. Once she finished confessing her dirt, she sat on the edge of the bed with tear-stained cheeks and let out a huge sigh of relief saying, "Okay, Mommy, I think that's all of my secrets."

I pulled her into my lap without hesitation and covered her in my embrace. I told her a story about my failures, revealing a side of my heart she had never seen before. I assured her that she wasn't a bad little girl by helping her understand that it's all part of growing into her identity. Once she had settled down, and I made sure she was comforted, I tucked her into bed and told her goodnight.

I didn't think much about it afterward and began to go about my nightly routine. But while standing in my bathroom taking off my makeup, I heard a little voice come into the room. "Mommy?" I looked over to see Kins standing in the doorway crying as she looked at me.

"Baby, what's wrong? Why are you crying?"

All of a sudden, she ran over to me, wrapped her arms around my waist and cried out, "I love you! I never want to leave you! I want to live with you until I'm old!"

Friends, I tell you this story from the heart of a mother. No secret my child could ever confess would keep me from believing in who I know she can be. Her ability to sit in a room with me and uncover her heart brought a new understanding to her of who I am as "Mom." She got to see a new side of me as I revealed a part of my story that she never knew existed. And in that moment, my words brought freedom from shame and guilt to her life.

If a child can experience love and peace on that level, from someone who has pages of dirt to read from, then how much more can we experience freedom, in the midst of our dirt, from a loving Father? What if I told you that Jesus didn't come to bring another religion, but he came to restore relationship with his children? What if I told you that rules, regulations, ritual, and routine were established long before Jesus was ever born? What if I told you that he came to bring an intentional understanding of who the Father is, beyond our conventional doctrine? What if you understood that your relationship with God cannot be cultivated unless you're willing to uncover areas of your heart that you're scared to expose? How would understanding that ALL your sins have been forgiven—before you ever had a chance to commit them (see John 1:29)—change the way you embrace your destiny?

When you begin to walk in the freedom of your righteousness in Christ (see Romans 3:22), you can come confidently into his presence knowing that your dirt does not define you, and that it can bring destiny to your life. That's where you'll find the heart of a loving Father. That's where he'll reveal a side of himself that you never knew existed. That's where you'll realize that he's not angry at you, and that he'll always accept you with arms open wide and a love that runs deep.

You cannot embrace your destiny until you learn—while being unfiltered—to embrace who you are in his presence. It's then, and only then, that he'll begin to uncover the lies that have marked your life and teach you who you truly are.

Confession

I did *all* the things religion told me not to do, but I still saw promise fulfilled in my life.

Truth

The fulfillment behind his word comes when you stop denying that you're flesh and blood and start allowing your spirit-man the ability to course-correct your posture when you get off track.

Journal entry
March 31, 2018

Hello,

This past year has been a process of teaching my heart how to sing in the midst of sorrow; it has been a dance of finding rhythm even in the midst of sour notes. During this chaos, I've sat wide-eyed in wonder of the Father and watched him gently create beauty with the wreckage.

I continue to learn, and watch in amazement, as I wait and take a moment to breathe. I know his love is filled with endless grace toward me, and I rest in that ... even when life tries to tell me otherwise.

I'm finding that the more the dust settles, and the air begins to clear, the more I find myself sorting through the pieces of my heart with the Father. It never stops. And for that I'm grateful because I'm realizing that he's creating space so I can learn to dance in the rhythm of his grace.

I've never known grace like this before. I used to be bound to religion in ways that kept me rebellious to his love. But I've found that his grace is endless. It never fails. It covers my wreckage. It says yes when my answer is no. It waits for me, no matter how long I take. It doesn't hesitate. It never runs dry. It follows me faithfully. It moves when I can't and takes my hand when my fingers fail to reach. It finds me when I'm blind. It calls for me when I'm lost. It marks me with its love. Its requirements are none. It doesn't condemn. It says I'm enough. It changes my name. It gives me rest. It erases my shame and replaces guilt. It is sufficient. It is ever-present.

And most of all, I've found that his grace is mine.

Today I danced in the rhythm of his grace, and I was proud. The pieces of my heart aren't done being sorted through; that became evident when a woman approached me at an Easter egg hunt today. She told me how much she admired my ministry and my love for the Father, and then she began to let me know of an affair she'd had with my ex-husband while he was still married to me.

Her words were gentle and full of sincerity. She asked for my forgiveness and said she'd had no idea we were married. I don't know if that's the truth, but regardless, I applauded her ability to look me in the eyes and confess.

In that moment, endless grace began to lead my feet as I danced over the situation with love, forgiveness, and ministry. I encouraged her to let it go and let God heal her heart, while he deals with my ex. I looked her in the eyes and told her that I forgive her ... and that the past is in the past. I prayed for her heart to heal, and I reminded her that broken people search to break others when they don't know how to become whole in Christ.

Today, grace gave me the ability to embrace this woman with a hug of forgiveness as I invited her to come celebrate the love of Jesus for Easter celebration tomorrow morning at my church. Once I ministered to her and we got done talking, she snapped a picture with me and again let me know how much she admires the love I have for God and how sorry she is. When I walked away from that field with my daughters in tow, I had a better understanding of what it looks like to truly love your enemies.

A whirlwind of emotions began to flood my brain as I got in the car, but the biggest one was the faithfulness of the Father and his love and grace toward me. He has protected me, even when I didn't know I was being protected. He has allowed rejection to be my deliverance. He knew of the secret things before I ever had a clue as to what was going on. He has brought restoration amidst devastation. He has absolutely created with the chaos, and it's beautiful.

My sweet fiancé (Brandon) never ceases to show me the Father's heart and love. When I dropped the girls off with my mom, I called him crying as I processed this experience. Feelings of betrayal, hurt, and rejection tried to rear their ugly head. I could barely speak as I sobbed into the phone, "I feel so dirty. How could he have multiple affairs with different women while still making love to me during that time in our marriage? And I had no clue! Why didn't I know?"

Bran is so patient. He sat there, listened, and loved on me while gently reminding me of my future. He never shamed me for feeling the way I felt, and he never cut me off while expressing my heart. I thought to myself, *Thank you, Father, for allowing this wreckage that's full of pain, because it allowed me to find a man that's full of purpose. You always have a plan, even when I can't see it clearly.*" After I was done, Bran reminded me of who I am in Christ: I am not dirty and distant; I am clean and close. He allowed me to see that this is all part of my story, and there's substance here to set others free with the love of Jesus.

I am not dirty and distant; I am clean and close.

So today is a victory. I have clearly danced in grace, with the rhythm of the Father's heart, and only stumbled a little. I haven't yet mastered his steps completely, but I'm proud to say I got on the dance floor and followed his lead … even if I did shed a few tears while processing the experience of it all.

I know his grace is sufficient, and I will continue to learn the movement of his love.

Alissa

Chapter 13: *Grace*

I had an appointment with my doctor this morning; it was a typical pre-op appointment. We discussed all the dos and don'ts for the days leading up to my surgery next Tuesday. I brought my computer with me to do some editing while I sat in the waiting room, and I found myself learning the grace dance all over again as I read through the pages of this book.

Friend, can I tell you that this journey you're on will never stop? Once you arrive at a place of promise, you'll find that you're continuously being prepared for the next phase of your destiny. Even through all the healing, sorting, restoration, and promise that's been fulfilled in my life, I find myself standing on a new road and covered in

.

dirt.

This month marks twelve solid months of actively trying as we wait for the promise of a child. I honestly never thought infertility would be a part of our story, but then again, I never thought my story would contain any of the horrible things I've had to walk through. Still, I walk on because I know God is faithful.

Conceiving my girls couldn't have been an easier task for me. With one decision made, one try on the whim of a moment, and one pregnancy test, my oldest daughter made her presence known in my life. I don't think I ever even had a chance to process the fact that I was trying for a baby before I found that it wasn't the flu making me barf every morning—I had a child growing in my belly instead.

My youngest was a tad bit different though. She gave me four months to prepare my mind for pregnancy before the digital pee stick lit up with the word "pregnant" on the front. I remember sitting down with my parents that month to ask them to pray with me because I didn't understand why it was taking so long to get pregnant. Now looking back, I laugh. Four months is nothing compared to a year. I'd give anything for that to be my problem today.

Both of my girls were conceived in different years, but during the same month and on the same week. So they had due dates only five days apart, and I often joked that my fertile month was obviously September—and I'd be lying if I said my hopes weren't high when September rolled around last year for Bran and me. When the test showed up negative, my heart sank. Once again, it was abundantly clear that we weren't pregnant.

Trying for baby number three has been vastly different than my other two tries. The past twelve months were filled with multiple phone apps tracking my cycle, fertility schedules to follow, ovulation tests to take, and a stack of pregnancy tests showing us nothing more than that dreaded single line every time. My husband started taking natural supplements and essential oils to help with his sperm health, and I've been downing vitamins and prenatal pills like candy.

Friends and family constantly shower us with advice on what to do and what not to do (as if I've never conceived children before and there's some magic formula we haven't tried yet). We've sat and listened to one conversation after another, hearing people say things like, "Just relax. When you try too hard you hinder things." Or, "Have fun trying! When you enjoy it, you'll find that it will happen faster." Or, "Just stop trying. That's usually when it happens." And let's not forget the best one, "Maybe it's not God's timing. You need to just let it go and know that it will happen when it's supposed to happen."

You know what? I can genuinely say, from the bottom of my heart, that we've taken their advice … all of it, but we're still not pregnant.

Now we've gone from following that advice to practicing old wives' tales—like the one that told me to lay in bed with my legs up for twenty minutes after sex because somehow that's supposed to increase my chances of pregnancy (as if I have nothing better to do with my life). My poor husband has even gotten in on the action by using frozen peas fifteen minutes before we do the baby dance; they say it's supposed to cool the swimmers off so they can move faster. And as you can imagine, nothing makes you feel more manly than sticking frozen bags of food to your goods right before having sex.

With beach houses, trips to Canada for ministry, and cruise ships, we let go and had fun in light-hearted attempts to let nature take its place while we enjoyed the practice. Some months, we followed the little app on my calendar to a T, while other months we didn't. Many months, my period would come right on time, but sometimes it would come late. And there were even a couple of months where it didn't show up at all. Still, the test read "not pregnant," and one evil, little line continued to stare us in the face.

When nothing seemed to be working for us, we decided to make doctor's appointments and received strict instructions to follow afterward. Brandon's process included semen collections and more dos and don'ts—like not wearing tight boxers, avoiding hot tubs, and taking certain meds. My process included sonograms to measure my ovaries and check for ovulation while also being given a strict sex schedule to follow during each of my cycles (how romantic).

With every passing month, we've shed tears, experienced meltdowns, and watched those around us get pregnant while we've waited. So with a bottle of wine and a bag of chocolates, I found myself lying in bed one night after my cycle started (once again). I'd poured another glass and began to count. Not three, not five, not eight, but *fifteen* friends of mine had gotten pregnant during the time we'd been trying for baby Holt. One of those fifteen included my sister who had a nine-month-old at the time. She got to do the whole "Christmas announcement" thing that I so longed to do but didn't get to partake in.

Nothing makes you angrier than wanting so badly to be happy for people while being sad for yourself. The truth is that I *am* happy. I've celebrated others, attended their gender reveal parties and baby showers, and can genuinely say I'm thrilled for each and every one of them. My heart leaps for them when they tell me the news.

But still, all my excitement for them didn't stop me from running out of my dear friends' house at their gender reveal party this past month. With pink confetti flying through the air and the sound of everyone screaming, "It's a girl!" my smile began to shift to tears when they began passing around sonogram pictures of the sweet, little human growing inside her belly. (Oh, how my heart aches for that.) It hit me like a ton of bricks and without any warning. *This friend began trying for a baby at the same time as me, and now she has a gender, a name, and a due date while my womb remains empty.* As I looked at those sonogram pictures, my heart began to cry out in my chest, and in the midst of celebrating a friend, I found myself darting out of the room to catch a breather.

This has been one of the hardest roads I've ever had to walk down, but knowing that Bran and I are walking it hand in hand makes it a little easier. We've had the opportunity to learn faith from a new perspective, and it has shown us the importance of celebrating others while we claim *our* promise. There's nothing that screams, "I will not be defeated!"

more than embracing those who have received the same promise you're waiting on and allowing it to bring you hope for your tomorrow.

The path we're on right now shows surgery, but the hope is that it'll increase our chances of conceiving a child. Our doctor will perform a D&C (dilation and curettage of the uterus) to give a clean slate for Bran's boys to swim through, and he'll remove any scar tissue I have from my previous C-sections. And the fact is, I hate surgery, but sometimes the grace dance requires doing things you don't necessarily want to do in order to get you where you need to go.

One of Bran's testimonies is that he not only kept his virginity by waiting thirty-three years for his good thing (aka me), but God gave him one of his biggest desires in life by allowing him to be a dad to my two daughters.

For his first Father's Day, the girls picked out his gifts all on their own, and their choices melted my heart. Kins picked out a Georgia Bulldogs card that read "Number One Dad" on the front, with a golden "Best Dad" pin attached. Rory picked out a wooden sign that read "World's Best Dad" for him to put in his office. I couldn't help but smile at the faithfulness of God for giving them a man they love so much and can trust with their heart.

I wanted nothing more than to give him a positive pregnancy test that month. Instead, I gave my honey a black baby hat with the word

"Holt" embroidered on the band in white. It came with a hand-written card confessing to him that I'd initially bought the hat six months prior and had planned to give it to him when I found out we were pregnant. With every passing month and every negative test staring me in the face, I'd begun to pray, and I felt in my heart that I was to give Brandon the hat in faith for us to pray over as we wait for our child to arrive. Without hesitation, we laid hands on that hat and anointed it with oil as we called forth our son by name. Since then, it's sat on our nightstand as a reminder to not grow weary while we wait and to have confidence in the knowing that our promise is on the way. Any time we begin to feel the dream of our child die, we start prophesying over our present circumstance by declaring the promise of God's Word to be true.

You will be blessed more than any other people; none of your men or women will be childless. (Deuteronomy 7:14)

And by faith even Sarah, who was past childbearing age, was enabled to bear children because she considered him faithful who had made the promise. (Hebrews 11:11)

This season has reminded me of the time in my life where I wore a hoody that marked me with abandonment. That was the place where I learned to speak healing over my life while posturing myself in faith. It was where I found that my voice has power as I called forth a husband who would bring purpose to my destiny. I allowed myself grace to feel, but I didn't allow my feelings to overtake my faith. Today I found myself in that place once more as I sat in an office preparing for surgery, with hopes that this will help us conceive our son. Through it all, I haven't allowed what I see to shake what I believe. I simply speak the Word of God and know that he is faithful to keep his promises.

I allowed myself grace to feel, but I didn't allow my feelings to overtake my faith.

Know what I've learned to be true about faith? It's the voice that speaks to my destiny, but it's absent without the cord of grace allowing it to be heard. Listen, friend, a voice cannot be heard unless it has vocal cords to form its sound. If something is worth speaking, then both must work together in order for sound to go forth and be heard.

What am I saying exactly? I'm saying that faith and grace go hand in hand, and until we learn to lace fingers with them both, we'll never embrace the fullness of what God has for our lives.

Confession #13: I lived for years with my faith on mute, when I thought I had a megaphone in my hand.

Being raised in a Word of Faith family has given me a strong understanding of what it looks like to not only *walk* by faith but to *speak* by faith when you're still waiting to see the evidence of what you're believing for. But, for years, it was hit-and-miss with what I saw come to pass in my life. I personally believe I experienced that because of the direct connection to the unspoken warzone that's forever been between the Faith and Grace movements. Although I was raised with a great understanding of faith, my knowledge of grace was quite weak. That placed me in a posture of *doing* instead of understanding that it's already *done*. It kept me in a position of *wanting* instead of realizing that Jesus, on the cross, *won* the victory for all my needs.

I'll never understand why biblical foundations become such taboo subjects within the church and amongst believers. The Faith movement is associated with people who are known for their name it and claim it, blab it and grab it, holier-than-thou lifestyle. While the Grace movement has become smeared with an identity that marks people as greasy-grace believers who have no convictions for how they live their life and claim freedom as their excuse card.

For the love of coffee, make the madness stop!
Friend, I'm here to unfilter this issue for you, and I hope you'll read my words loud and clear. Faith and grace were never meant to be a MOVEMENT in and of themselves—they were meant to be a MARRIAGE that intertwines. For too long, we've made a fist out of faith and a game out of grace, and we've found ourselves standing in the ring fighting with each other over what *movement* brings God more glory and satisfaction.

Faith and grace were meant to be a marriage

that intertwines.

I've stood and watched as we've blasted pastors, ripped hearts apart, divided churches, and thrown away books that don't meet the standards of whichever side of the ring we're standing on. The sad part is that we've never thought twice about the fact that maybe the fist of faith was made to perfectly fit into the glove of grace! Maybe the two weren't meant to fight against each other but were perfectly fashioned to lock hands with each other and work *together* to find restoration in the ring.

For it is by grace you have been saved, through faith—and this is

not from yourselves, it is the gift of God. (Ephesians 2:8)

Hear this, the requirement for salvation isn't found in the ability to be dirt(sin)-free. In fact, it's not found within the ability to name it and claim it through faith either. Nor is it found in your right to smear greasy grace across your name. The requirement for salvation is found when the glove meets the fist by posturing itself in a position to fight this battle we call "life" TOGETHER.

In other words, the only way you can receive salvation is by going through both grace and faith at the same time. What does that look like exactly? It's something like this: grace is God's job; faith is your job. Which is a lot like the saying, "You do what you can, and God will do what you can't." Salvation is a perfect illustration of what that looks like; grace and faith collide and find you in the midst of your dirt. There's nothing you can do to deserve the grace he has freely given you, but there's only one way you can receive it. You have to activate your faith in order to claim what he says is yours.

Friend, you may think you have a megaphone in your hand while you spout all the scriptures, declarations, and positive vibes into the atmosphere, but your faith will remain on mute until you recognize that your works don't determine your ability to receive your promise. The voice of faith cannot be heard without the chord of grace. God doesn't show his grace toward you in response to your faith; your faith is a response to the grace of God and what he's already given you. Stop trying to manipulate the promise of his Word by shouting Scripture, and realize, instead, that he's already made every promise in his Word available through salvation. His grace met your faith at the altar, and Jesus sealed every bit of purpose for your life when he hung on the cross and said, "It is done."

The voice of faith cannot be heard without the chord of grace.

So what do you do after you've gone through the process toward promise? What do you do after you've dug deep by sorting through the pieces and allowing God to rebuild you? What takes place after you claim your seat of destiny during the pause of the process? How do you move forward from there?

Well, this is one of the easier parts of your journey. This is where you lock hands with grace by allowing God to do his part, and you activate your faith by continuing to do your part! This is where you step into the ring with confidence because you know that the fight you're in right now—the fight for seeing promise fulfilled in your life—has been set up for *purpose* and not for *pain*! This moment is nothing more than another opportunity to fight like hell and watch grace carry you through the final knockout punch. And guess what?

YOU WIN!

From here on out, you won't try to make things happen on your own. From here on out, you'll give yourself some grace to feel, lean on the Father, and trust in his timing. No longer will you carry the burden of proving yourself in order to possess the thing you're waiting for. No, you'll learn to do the grace dance by following his lead. By following the lead of a loving father and locking hands with him, you'll be able to take steps in faith—one at a time.

This is where God's grace is sufficient, and his timing is perfect.

Confession

I lived for years with my faith on mute, when I thought I had a megaphone in my hand.

Truth

God doesn't show his grace toward you in response to your faith; your faith is a response to the grace of God and what he has already given you.

Journal entry
April 19, 2018

Hello,

"I'm confident your faithfulness will see me through." —Steffany
Gretzinger

The strength I discover in the Father's faithfulness, when I am weak,
is beyond me. No matter how hard I seem to get knocked out, his love is
always there to cover me with enough grace to get back up.

Grace.

That word is so prominent in this season of my life. It seems like
I've nearly written an entire book about it throughout this past year. And
what I'm learning is that, without grace, my faith cannot strive. Without
grace, my love cannot grow. Without grace, my mind can't be renewed.
And without grace, true repentance can't take place. Grace is the very life
that breathes in the midst of despair.

Grace is the very life that breathes in the

midst of despair.

I recall an entry I wrote back in July of last year. It was right about the time I felt complete peace in my decision to file for divorce. Some of the words I'd penned read:

> Today I feel different. It's as if I was fighting in the ring and
>
> giving it my all; I was using all my strength and was a bloody
>
> mess, but today I feel like the fight is over. I feel like I'm ready to
>
> start cleaning up the bloodstains, and now I can prepare myself to
>
> step out of the ring. There's peace to let go of this marriage …
>
> and guess what? I'm okay. I'm ready to put the gloves down and
>
> let the wounds heal.

These past two weeks feel as though I've been tagged back in for every fight I could possibly battle. Except this time, the battle is in my mind with things like depression, worry, fear, trust, anger, health, and finances. As I'm fighting, my mind is in the ring. It's like the bell has rung, and one fight after another has begun. The battle of anger and hate began to rage again when more lies and unfaithfulness surfaced about even more affairs that took place during my previous marriage. When that happened, the battle of feeling used and dirty began to feed insecurities I haven't felt since I was raped nearly thirteen years ago. And from there, it felt as though I spun my way into a fight of trust. What if Bran hurts me? What if he cheats like my ex-husband? What if he leaves the girls and me? What if he doesn't want me once we marry and he gets the chance to live with me?

Surprise!

That tagged me in for a battle with rejection and abandonment. I felt alone because Bran isn't here with me physically and I miss him dearly. We've been away from each other for nearly six weeks, and I hate it. Then once I felt like I'd finally gotten a grip on my mind and was back up on my feet again, the battle for my health began. Abnormal tests from my OB-GYN started it all, and a week later, I found myself in serious pain in my belly and ovaries, which landed me in the ER ... only to learn that I needed an emergency appendectomy.

Tag!

I was back in the ring and began to fight rejection and loneliness all over again. All of it stemmed from old wounds resurfacing from my ex-husband. He'd never really taken care of me during previous surgeries and illnesses—my Dad always stepped in.

Even though Bran covers me in love, prayer, attention, care, affirmation, grace, and leadership, I still feel alone because my heart is used to being alone in sickness. I know I'm not emotionally alone and my family is here, but I'm physically not with Brandon, and this health issue pulled up past emotions from previous experiences with illness. ... So here I am, fighting depression. Wanting Bran to be here with me. Hating distance.

Ding, ding, ding!

It's been one bell after another. One fight after another. One swing after another. It's as though I've been stuck in my mind and unable to win. With a call from my doctor yesterday, I heard the chime of the bell once more. A fight against fear for my health has now begun. The report says my appendix had what looked to be two stones inside of it. After having the lab test them, they found that they weren't stones after all. ... In fact, they were two cancerous tumors.

Thus starts the fight of faith because the devil is a liar, and I refuse to believe this report.

And can I just say that the gloves are on tight this round? A righteous anger has hit me, and I'm ready to continue fighting until I win! My mind has become a ring that I'm far too familiar with lately, and to be honest, I'm tired. I'm tired of being defeated. Tired of losing my breath in certain areas of my life. I'm tired of getting knocked down and having to find the strength to swing again.

Over the last year, I've conquered my mind in the areas of defeat, insecurity, intimidation, hurt, pain, fear, rejection, abandonment, and loneliness. Now I have to understand that this is *not* my fight and I've *already won* through Christ!

It is done!

No matter what I see. No matter what I feel. No matter what I hear. IT IS FINISHED and I WILL FIGHT until I see it manifest in my life. There's nothing broken, nothing missing, nothing lost. The ring may be in my mind right now, and the battle may be on, but as I've said daily for a year now, "I refuse to lose!"

So, Father, tag me in. I know I have the strength to win this one. We're eight days away from my wedding, but I will fight in white if I have to.

Alissa

Chapter 14: *You*

This week has been quite eventful for the Holt household.
We're officially back home after evacuating Savannah due to Hurricane
Dorian. And I've learned that no matter how much entertainment you
pack for your kids, they still want **YOU** to entertain them. With toys,
electronics, movies, and art supplies crammed into bags, I'd thought for
sure that there would be zero reason for boredom over the few days we'd
be gone. Man, oh man, was I wrong.

  With a trip to Atlanta, and four days of being cooped up in a family
member's home, we made the decision to get out and do something fun.
The kids have never been to a science museum before, and Cartersville
had one that was top-notch. So we decided to check it out. Surely a

planetarium, dinosaur gallery, and the ability to pan for gems and dig for fossils would keep these kids from wanting our phones and electronics every two seconds (not likely)!

With one goal in mind (to have some fun), I quickly found that the joke was on me as we approached the king himself ... Mr. T-Rex. I didn't realize it at the moment, but the picture I'd take of my girls standing underneath this monster skeleton would remind me of a huge life lesson I've put into practice daily over the last few years.

So picture this, two little human beings standing underneath a killing machine (aka Mr. T-Rex) that's big enough to make those humans look like ants. All the while, this mommy is standing on the sidelines with her phone so I can capture whatever pose they make as they confront this monstrosity of a creature. I didn't quite recognize their postures in the picture until later that day, but it perfectly captured what it looks like to stand in the midst of adversity and choose how we want to view it.

As I looked back on the snapshot, I noticed that one child had her hands held high, protecting her face, as she displayed a look of terror and cowered down under the mouth of the dino. But my other child crouched down and showed her teeth, as if she was "rawring" right back at him, and her hands were positioned to fight as she looked him straight in the face!

When I saw the picture, my immediate thought was that this is how *filtered* and *unfiltered* look, side by side, while staring the monster we call "life" straight in the face.

Confession #14: Fear used to filter the way I saw life, and it

kept me paralyzed to purpose.

"Why do bad things happen to good people?" That's a question I get asked over and over again in ministry. I used to ask that question myself. That is, until the doctors discovered cancer in my body. That's when I began to question just who the monster really is. Is it the thing I'm facing, or is it the God I'm serving? Does the bad have anything to do with the good I do in my life, or is God just a mean God who loves to test our humanity?

Just when restoration found its way back into my life and all the pieces began to fall back into place, it seemed like every ounce of wind was knocked out of me with only eight days left in the countdown for my wedding. What should have been a time of celebration became filtered with the fear of chemo. All the sudden, everything I'd seen rebuilt and restored became masked with the possibility of it ending before it ever truly began. Fear paralyzed my vision from seeing purpose and victory in my future.

I'll never forget sitting on the town-square bench as I called to gently break the news to Bran. He was in Georgia that week getting our home in order, and I was in Arkansas packing boxes as the girls and I prepared to move. Through our tears, we allowed each other grace to feel the reality of where we were in that moment, but we ended the call by activating our faith and declaring the promise that by his stripes I am healed (see Isaiah 53:5, NKJV).

When we got off the phone, I immediately drove to my house and pulled out my guitar to sing Elevation Worship's lyrics, "His promise still stands. Great is His faithfulness ... faithfulness. I'm still in his hands. This is my confidence, you've never failed me yet." And without even realizing it, my fiancé was sixteen hours away, in his office, playing the same song on his piano and singing the same lyrics. Even though we were miles apart and had no clue what the other was doing, something happened for us in that moment. We experienced the power behind overcoming. And, friend, I'm here to tell you that the power you're waiting for starts with YOU. How is that possible exactly? How does the responsibility to overcome rest on you and your shoulders? Let's read:

They triumphed over him by the *blood of the Lamb* and by the *word of their testimony*; they did not love their lives so much as to shrink from death. (Revelation 12:11, emphasis added)

Let me ask you today, what kind of death are you facing in your life? Is it the possibility of cancer? Is it the end of a marriage? Is it bankruptcy? Are you dealing with the end of a chapter and find yourself starting over? What does the monster in front of you look like? Once you've put a face to that thing, ask yourself this, How am I posturing myself while I face it?

Are your hands held high as you take cover and paralyze your purpose with fear, or are you taking the posture to fight back as you look it in the eyes and say, "I overcome!"

Friend, I cannot say this loud enough. YOU are the answer to victory in your life because Jesus already did everything he came to do!

Why is it that you're still waiting on him to show up? His part was completed on the cross, and he has already covered you in grace to win this battle. Stop waiting on him! Start to recognize that he's waiting on you to utilize everything you have inside of you (see Acts 17:28) to CONQUER THE MONSTER that's in front of you!

If Jesus already declared, "It is finished," then what's left to be done? You've already won this battle through him! It's time for you to activate the faith inside of you that says, "If God said it, then I believe it. And if I believe it, then I receive it!" Nothing is settled in your life until you make up your mind! Okay, so the odds are stacked against you? So what! Where's your mind at? Wherever your mind is, so will your faith be, and fear and faith cannot be in your mouth at the same time! It's impossible.

Fear and faith cannot be in your mouth at the same time!

I like to put it like this, Y.O.U. = YOU OVERCOME, UNFILTERED. Do you want to know how you do that? You do that by not allowing fear to filter an ending to your story that's not yours to write! You overcome by unfiltering the lies of your situation with the truth of

God's Word. That unfiltering happens by declaring *ahead of time* (before you see it as a reality) what it is that God says about you. Your testimony is found in your MOUTH, with the words you speak, and by the blood of Jesus, you can (and will) overcome!

When I received the call saying, "You have cancer in your body, and it very well might still be there," my heart sank. But my faith stood strong. That night, I found myself pacing the same floors I'd paced when I couldn't see even a glimpse of restoration in my future. They were the same halls I'd walked down as I declared the goodness of God over my girls and myself when all I saw was destruction.

As I paced those floors and spoke faith over my life that night, I learned that restoration is a process that never stops, but it's a journey I must continue. I found that, to be restored, I must make a daily decision to be renewed.

re ·new[1]

rə 'n(y)oo͞

verb

1. Re-establish; repeat; give fresh life or strength to

2. Extend for a further period the validity of

3. Replace

re ·store[2]

rə ˈstôr

verb

1. Bring back; reinstate; return to a former condition, place, or position; repair or renovate so as to return it to its original condition; give back to the original owner or recipient

Listen, having experienced restoration (promise) in your life up until this point doesn't mean that you'll never have to be renewed in certain areas of your life again. In fact, it means that your responsibility to steward restoration is now *greater*, and you'll be required to go through seasons where you must renew your mind.

Do not conform to the pattern of this world, but be transformed

by the renewing of your mind. Then you will be able to test and

approve what God's will is—his good, pleasing and perfect will.

(Romans 12:2)

Despite every answered promise, I still found myself standing under a new monster, and its name was "cancer." I could have questioned God and his goodness when I received that phone call. I could have allowed my anger to cause more hell than healing during that moment. I could have paralyzed my purpose by allowing fear of the unknown to take me captive, but I didn't. I had a choice to make, guys, and it was going to determine my course. Would I posture myself with the filter of fear, or would I stand in faith, knowing that nothing catches God by surprise?

For me, the decision was easy. I'd been through too much fire to let cancer be the monster that took me out. Over the next few days, I pulled out every promise I had recorded on paper and every voice memo I had of me speaking victory over my life. I listened to them while I slept at night. I read them during my morning study time. I posted them on my mirrors and refrigerator. I reminded myself of who I am and what God has already done for me. I told myself this was nothing more than a plot twist to bring *purpose* to my tomorrow!

Only three days before I married my best friend, my phone rang with more news from the doctor. It was the call I'd been waiting for. The call that would determine what the fight looked like and what we'd do next. When my previous labs had come back, my surgeon made the executive decision to send my appendix and the tumors to a lab in Cleveland, Ohio. He wanted to be sure of two things:

1. If they were, indeed, cancerous.
2. Whether or not it had spread throughout my body.

The report confirmed that the tumors were cancerous, but it also showed that they were 100 percent contained within my appendix and no further treatment or follow ups would be needed. The doctor went on to say, "I wanted to give you the report now so you can enjoy your honeymoon! At this rate, you have a *long* life ahead of you.

Congratulations!"

Friends, this is the part of the story where I grab you by the face as your eyes lock with the words on these pages. You see, I went into the ER because I'd been having severe pain in my ovaries and could barely stand. Once I arrived, they performed a CAT scan that showed my appendix was inflamed and held two stones; that led them to believe it was fixing to rupture. I was immediately taken by ambulance and transferred to a hospital in Little Rock, two hours away, for an emergency appendectomy. From there, they sent my appendix to the lab because of how abnormal it looked, which led to the final results where the doctor's words pierced my heart and changed my life forever.

He said, "Ms. Powers, here's the thing. Your reports show that you never once had signs of appendicitis. Looking at the scans, your symptoms should have been accompanied with fever, severe abdominal pain, and throwing up. You had none of those symptoms, and we were all very curious about it because the scan showed that your appendix was very much abnormal and looked inflamed. ... Once we got in there, we saw that you had an ovarian cyst that had ruptured and caused lots of bleeding. From your reports, we see that you're on medication to keep that from happening but thank goodness it did! If it weren't for the pain you were in from the cyst, we would have never found the cancer in your appendix. Ms. Powers, this is what we call a freak discovery. A year from now, you would have been visiting us under far worse circumstances. The cancer would have spread, and you would have had to undergo treatment! Looks like you're blessed!"

How many times do we question the pain in our life and accuse God of being a monster when he's simply setting us up for destiny? From my view of life, all I saw were answered promises being ripped away from me because of the potential possibility of death. BUT GOD! Nothing takes him by surprise. He can see all the details that we don't even know exist. So hear me when I say there is *purpose* in your *pain*! If it weren't for God allowing me to develop a cyst (that resulted in surgery), I never would have had the opportunity to see the cancer removed from my body! What I viewed as destruction, God saw as restoration! He allowed pain to manifest in my life, not to be a mean Father, but to set me up for destiny by stopping death from stealing my purpose!

What I viewed as destruction, God saw as restoration!

What is it that you're facing right now? What pain are you defining as punishment, when God is simply positioning you for your promise? I know it makes zero sense at the moment, but just know that he doesn't waste a thing! He creates with chaos and restores from the rubble of life! Maybe the thing you hate so much right now is attached to your answered prayers. Trust him with the process and get your mind right! You overcome when you make a decision to keep faith in your mouth by declaring the ending before it ever happens! You carry the ability to either renew your mind or let it run wild with fear. Change your perspective and watch as God changes your position! Your ability to see what he has for you will require you to open your eyes to the truth of his Word.

Friend, your destiny cannot be stolen from you when the King has signed it. You *can* overcome because Christ has *already* overcome.

Confession

Fear used to filter the way I saw life, and it kept me paralyzed to purpose.

Truth

Y.O.U. = YOU OVERCOME, UNFILTERED. Fear and faith cannot be in your mouth at the same time!

Journal entry
November 3, 2018

Hello,

Vitamin "Sea" is just what I've needed. B and I recently came back
from our first cruise. We had the honor of being invited on board to lead
worship for a church that was taking a trip. I didn't realize how significant
this trip would be for me, but life is different, and my heart has found
new freedom. There's something about the sea that brings new direction
… or at least for me it did.

I saw a quote today, by Vincent van Gogh, that read, "The heart of
man is very much like the sea, it has its storms, it has its tides, and in its
depths it has its pearls too." I can truly say I've found pearls this week,
and I will cherish them for a lifetime.

The night before the cruise, I began to prepare my heart for
something I knew would be significant in my life. Over the past five
weeks, God has taken me through a detailed process of drowning out lies

that have tried to steal the restoration in my life. Through the process, I felt led to write letters of release to those who have wounded my heart in one way or another—including my rapist, my ex-husband, the women who were involved in the affairs, and even hurts that stem back to childhood and church. I felt in my heart that I was to take those letters on the cruise with me to release into the ocean, once and for all, as a defining moment signifying freedom from the lies I've carried around for too long.

Restoration truly is a process and a picture of creation. Something new can't be made until the old is torn down. In order to let go of what I've allowed to hold me back, I've had to revisit some pain in the last five weeks that I never wanted to encounter again.

With prayers, notes, letters, and voice memos to remind me of just how far I've come (and how much I'm letting go), I took some time to review it all—before the final goodbye—while I was flying into Miami from Oklahoma. In doing so, I came across a video on my phone from the beginning months of when my husband left me. My intention was to send him the video, but I never did. Instead, I used it as a tool to heal my heart. It was heartbreaking to watch, and it put me in tears as I sat on the plane. It was from such a horrible time in my life; depression, hurt, loneliness, anger, and uncertainty had followed me around daily. And the words and emotion of that video pierced my heart once more as I remembered where God has carried me from, and where he's placing me at now.

The cruise was beautiful with all the music, sounds, energy, entertainment, and food. The views were breathtaking, and the memories made were priceless. If ever I had a time of renewed love and refreshing with my husband, this would be it. We desperately needed that trip, and now it signifies a moment of freedom that will mark our lives forever.

On the last day of the cruise, we took the whole day to prepare for the moment I'd been waiting for. I would drown every lie that's kept me from fully dreaming of and possessing my destiny, once and for all. I sat on our balcony and watched the sun set as I read over the pain, pieces, emotions, and letters I'd taken time to sort through with the Father over the past month. And with tears streaming down my face, I wrote a final ending to the letter meant for my ex-husband and all the women he'd been with while we were married. It was a letter of release, and a declaration of forgiveness, as I signed it with a promise to myself that I would never EVER try to revive that pain again. I made a promise to my daughters that they'd never grow up with a mother who was broken and filled with trauma from her past, but that they'd have a mommy who is healed and whole through Christ. Once I was done with the letters, I signed my name, folded them up, and tucked them away until the moment they would drown in the ocean forever.

Later that evening, we got all dressed up for one more dinner together on board and decided to catch one last show for entertainment. And after all was said and done, the final moment of the cruise had arrived. The moment I'd been preparing for. It was the moment I'd been anticipating for over a month. It was *finally* time to release those letters into the ocean and turn the final tides of hurt to healing. It was finally time to drown the lies, once and for all, so I could see destiny fulfilled in my life! Apart from our wedding day, I don't think there's ever been a moment between Bran and I that brought more fulfillment than that.

With a misty sky and not a soul in sight, we walked out onto the deck with anticipation in our hearts. Nothing but ocean surrounded us, and I thought to myself, "This. Is. It." Bran held my hand while we listened to the crash of waves below and gazed over the side of the boat into the water beneath us, "Are you ready, love? This is forever. No more lies. … You are enough. You're going to change the world." He always has a way of putting my heart at ease and making me believe the best about myself.

In that moment, I don't think my heart could have been more ready. The only other time I yearned for such completion was when I took my groom to be my husband. As we watched the waves, Bran held me, and I listened while he prayed. He spoke life over my destiny and peace over my mind. He renounced lies that have marked me and declared healing and breakthrough over my heart. I don't think he could ever realize it, but he set me up for a time of healing to take place.

When he finished praying, I brought him to the chairs under the balcony and presented him with a letter of his own. Of course, he knew I was writing letters of release, but he had no idea he'd be receiving one too. It was vows of accountability that promised him a wife who is restored, healed, and whole. It was a declaration of destiny for our future and the commitment to never give up, no matter what we face in this lifetime. We sat curled up together on the deck as he read the letter. We cried, laughed, and thanked Jesus for that beautiful moment of change as I postured my heart for what would come next.

Walking to the edge of the ship with a huge pile of letters in my hand was exhilarating. For so many years, I'd allowed those areas to weigh me down in ways that had held me back from the purpose for my life. And over the past year, I'd seen such tremendous restoration take place, but to me, this was the final puzzle piece that would mark healing in my life for this particular season. So with our hands on the letters, we spoke freedom over the lies and completion over my life. One by one, I crumbled each letter up and handed it off to my husband as he threw it overboard to be consumed by the waves and never retrieved again. With each toss and every bit of emotion recorded on those pages, we spoke out loud, "This is forever. Never to be picked back up."

Once the last letter was released into the sea, Bran and I embraced each other as I laid my head on his chest and whispered, "It is done. I forgive you all, and I am healed."

With his hand on my chin, he looked me in the eyes and asked, "How do you feel, my love?"

To which I replied ... "Free."

Alissa

Chapter 15: *DNA*

Un·fil·tered[1]

ˌ ən ˈfiltərd

adjective

1. Not having been passed through a filter
2. Not having been toned down, censored, or edited

How do you unlayer yourself when you're used to wearing filters and feel that they bring you safety? Honestly, I've learned that most people are frightened by what's underneath it all. When it boils down to it, we're afraid of getting to know the unfiltered version of who we are because we don't fully know who that is. That's a scary place to be, friend, and remaining fearful of the unknown will keep you from stepping into the destiny for your life. Don't believe me? Ask me how I know.

For most of my life, the person in the mirror wasn't the person other people saw when they looked at me. I had created an image for myself that was toxic, and I watched as poison leaked into every aspect of my life. The reflection in the mirror brought me nothing more than masks. It created a distorted view of how I saw myself. And before I knew it, the person I perceived myself to be became a direct connection to the way I responded to life's circumstances and the people around me. It caused me years of dysfunction in my relationships, a lifetime of running from the purpose on my life, turmoil in my mind, and ultimately controlled the way I expressed my emotions. I was destructive in my character. I made excuses for my actions. My heart consistently ached for something more, but my mind kept me bound to the memory of yesterday.

With smiles painted on, and laughter that held an echo of sadness hidden within its core, I found that I was riddled with pain, rejection, low self-esteem, doubt, and worthlessness. When I stripped everything away, I found that the root cause of most of my issues lied within the fact that I felt unlovable and like I wasn't enough. Even with being raised in church and having been in full-time ministry for years of my life, I had no idea who I truly was. My encounter with religion kept me from truly experiencing a relationship with the Father, and it caused a tug-of-war effect that had me pulling at destiny while fighting to keep a grip on the distortion in my life.

To be frank, the process toward becoming unfiltered was downright terrifying, and it hurt like hell. I could have glamorized the journey for you, but promise is often found through pain, and the truth is an ugly road that requires work. Through it all, I found myself smack dab in the middle of a harsh reality—the lesson behind it was that sometimes you have to grieve the future you thought you had before you can ever grab ahold of the one you were created for.

In twelve short months, I had three name changes under my belt (my ex-husband's name, my maiden name, and my husband's name). And the truth I found hidden behind the process was that no matter how many times you change your name, your identity, your career, or your surroundings, you'll never find true joy and fulfillment unless Jesus is the source behind your promise. Even further than that, I found that *I am the answer* to my destiny—no one else.

Friend, I feel like we've processed through a whole lot of crap together during this book. And with this being the final chapter, I want to lay all the cards on the table for you. Yesterday I saw a quote on Pinterest that had me screaming, "YAS!" It read, "Sometimes sh** happens so that a shift can happen." Let me tell you, today, that sometimes you'll go through flames in order to melt off filters. Sometimes seasons end so that your story can finally begin. Sometimes you don't have answers for all of life's circumstances, but you'll always have assignment when it comes to your destiny.

I can't tell you why life has to be so hard, but I can tell you who holds all the pieces in his hand! There is *no* disappointing thing that can happen in your life to UNAPPOINT you from the thing you were created for!

What you need to walk away from this book knowing is that the completion of your promise relies solely on yourself, and the answer behind how to get there relies fully on the completed work of the cross! When Jesus hung on a tree, 100 percent #UNFILTERED and unashamed, he said three words that gave you the power to have everything you need to get through the worst kinds of hell.

Are you ready?

IT IS FINISHED!

What is "it" exactly? *It* could be defined as all the things that would say no to the destiny on your life. *It* would sound like all the lies that try to steal the identity of who you are in Christ, and what it is that he's done for you. *It* would look like all the tragedy, pain, circumstances, and obstacles that would stand in front of your promise and mock you by saying, "This will never be yours." *It* is everything that says you must do "x, y, z" in order to receive destiny. *It* is all the things that keep you *working* for *worth*. And *it* is the thing that will keep you running circles around your promise without ever laying hands on it.

To make it as clear as glass, *it* is everything the Old Covenant stood for. It's all the rules, regulations, rituals, and routines that wore people out in order for them to find worth. And if you're not careful, you'll revert to the old promises—the Old Covenant and all that was cancelled for the sake of *better* promises.

But IT has been FINISHED.

So you can stop making religion a job and start creating relationship with Jesus. Jesus came to free you of the filters by giving you the *finished* work of the cross! The moment he said, "It is finished," is the moment when the veil of filters was torn so that nothing could separate you from coming into the presence of the Father—just as you are! That's the moment when your sin collided with a Savior who marked you with a blood covenant and said *this* is forever!

To clean up the church talk, a blood covenant simply means that he sealed the promise for your purpose by dying for your destiny! A friend says something that pierces my heart every time: "He died your death so that you could live his life." I want to hit you with some Scripture because this is where you'll find freedom to become unfiltered and unashamed.

He died your death so that you can live his life.

Are you ready to remove some guilt, shame, pain, and burdens from your life? Let's read:

> For, on the one hand, a former commandment is *cancelled* because
>
> of its weakness and uselessness [because of its inability to justify
>
> the sinner before God] (*for the Law never made anything perfect*); while
>
> on the other hand a *better hope* is introduced through which we now
>
> continually *draw_near to God*. (Hebrews 7:18, AMP, emphasis added)

> But as it is, Christ has acquired a [priestly ministry], which is
>
> more excellent [than the old Levitical priestly ministry], for he is

the Mediator (Arbiter) of a *better covenant* [uniting God and man},

which has been enacted and rests on *better promises*. (Hebrews 8:6,

AMP, emphasis added)

When God speaks of *"A new covenant,"* he makes the first one obsolete.

And whatever is becoming obsolete (out of use, annulled) and

growing old is ready to disappear. (Hebrews 8:13, AMP, emphasis

added)

Here's the good news, friend. You are free from the law because a *better promise* has been made! Jesus cancelled everything that said we have to amount up to a certain standard of "holiness" in order to be *destined*. When Christ chose to hang for the sake of our hearts, he made a way for us to unite with the Father without fear of the dirt in our lives. This is not "Alissa's opinion." This is Scripture that has stood the test of time for centuries, and more to come.

So hear me, it doesn't matter what your situation looks like. You have the hope of Christ because he has already overcome for you! He made a way out of the trouble you're in by taking upon himself all of the shame, guilt, and bondage that comes with it. You don't have to do anything to earn it, and you don't have to break your back to prove that you're worthy. Your only requirement is to believe. That's it. One word. Not a list of rules or standards that are too hard to keep. All you have to do is believe.

Remember this scripture that we touched on earlier:

For God so [greatly] loved and dearly prized the world, that he [even] gave his [One and] only begotten Son, so that *whoever believes* and trusts in him [as Savior] *shall not perish, but have eternal life*. (John 3:16, AMP, emphasis added)

You see, filtered fashion began in the garden when Adam and Eve decided to cover up their shame with leaves. Jesus made the decision, in another garden, to unfilter the shame of sin by the sacrifice of his blood. Where does that leave us? It leaves us right here with the knowing that our job isn't to cover up our dirt. It leaves us with the understanding that it's not our responsibility to sacrifice ourselves for the sake of salvation. That's already been done!

Our job lies completely within our ability to *believe*!

What if I told you that your biggest downfall from here on out will boil down to that one thing? I'm continually amazed at the number of believers in the Christian circle who don't BELIEVE. We say one thing with our mouths, but we live in fear that we're not enough and that promise isn't ours. I suppose that's why we don't see the fulfillment of destiny in our lives at the rate we should as children of God. Our biggest job is to believe, but that's the area we struggle in the most.

When I came across this scripture, many years ago, I realized that everything the Word says I can have is connected to one thing—my ability to believe. Let's read:

Do you not *believe* that I am in the Father, and the Father is in me? The words I say to you I do not say on my own initiative or authority, but the Father, abiding continually in me, does his works [his attesting miracles and acts of power]. *Believe* me that I am in the Father and the Father is in me; otherwise *believe* [me] because of the [very] works themselves [which you have witnessed]. I assure you and most solemnly say to you, anyone who *believes* in me [as Savior] will also do the things that I do; and he will do even greater things than these [in extent and outreach], because I am going to the Father. And I will do whatever you ask in my name [as my representative], this I will do, so that the Father may be glorified and celebrated in the Son. If you ask me anything in my name [as my representative], I will do it.

If you [really] love me, you will keep and obey my commandments. (John 14:10-15, AMP, emphasis added)

What did he command us to do in this scripture? Look closely. He didn't say he commands us to not partake in a list of sins. He didn't give us a detailed rulebook to record religious tally marks in as we complete rituals and stay far away from sin. No, what he commanded us to do is to BELIEVE! He said it four times here alone. *Believe in me*! *Believe I am*! *Believe because of what I've done*! Jesus is clear about several things here.

1. We are representatives of him.
2. We must believe.
3. Believing will unlock our ability to do what he did and *even greater* works!

That leaves us with three questions. What do you do when you feel like you can't believe? What happens when you feel like you don't know how to believe? What happens when you feel like you don't have what it takes to find the strength to push through despite the pain?

I've found myself in that place so many times throughout my story. I've shared with you my tips and tricks for pushing record while on the mountaintops so you can push play during the moments of valleys. I've shared with you declarations and scriptures that I personally spoke over my life daily—I've even recorded them in the back of this book for you to have for your daily use.

Still, the questions remain.

Let me tell you, today, that you can do all the unfiltering, sorting, trusting, building, and digging that you want, but if you don't understand your design, you will never be able to touch your destiny. Knowing who it is that you are, and *whose* you are, is the key behind walking through the dirt of your life and embracing the destiny that was created for you.

If you don't understand your design, you will never be able to touch your destiny.

I do devotionals with my daughters every single morning while we sit in the school car line waiting for the building to open. Yesterday morning, I opened up a new plan with them on the YouVersion app; it was all about learning how to pray and the power they have to talk to Jesus. This particular lesson was on repentance, and a video came along with it to watch. While I sat there listening to the child on the video explain what repentance was and how it looked, my spirit cringed. They had a picture of Jesus standing in the middle of the screen and a picture of "you" that looked like a car. As they explained repentance, they showed the car moving toward Jesus, "With every good thing you do, and every commandment kept, you will move closer to Jesus. But with every sin you do, and every bad thing you allow into your life, you will move further from Jesus." We watched the car as they explained the idea that you can move closer to him if you keep all the rules, commandments, and do good things. Then all the sudden, the car turned around and began to drive away as they explained how you get further and further away from Jesus when you behave badly, sin, and don't show your love for him.

What they said next made me so angry, "The further you go away from Christ when you sin, the longer your journey back to him will become. You can repent from your sin and come back to Christ at any time, but the journey will be longer and will take more time to get back to where you were before you turned away." The entire lesson was ultimately all about how *doing* gets you destiny, and how *dirt* keeps you from destiny.

If I haven't articulated it enough throughout this book, let me squash that lie once and for all!

Your ability to *do* doesn't have any bearings on your ability to get back to Christ. Salvation isn't something you lose and then fight to regain. It's something that's yours, and it forever remains available for you to walk in. The moment you repent—remember, that means renewing your thinking, not just saying you're sorry—is the moment Christ will meet you, right where you're at! It doesn't take a longer time for you to find him again. In fact, the Word says that he will REDEEM the time lost by meeting you where you are. He is a restorer of all that is lost (see Deuteronomy 30:3-4, MSG), and he brings purpose, not punishment, to the broken pieces of your life!

We have to stop thinking that God is an angry king sitting on a throne, waiting for us to fall so he can bring judgment to our lives. He's so much better than that! He's a loving Father who wants nothing more than for us to walk in the fullness of life *right now,* even while we're dirty. Fun fact: the phrase "eternal life" is mentioned forty-one times in the

New Testament. And if it was worth repeating, then it must be pretty important for us to understand.

Confession #15: From the time I was a child, the phrase "eternal life" was equated to Heaven.

But my question has been, What does that leave us with while we're here on planet Earth?

I'll tell you where it leaves us. It leaves us waiting for promise. It leaves us thinking that every reward is in heavenly places, and that the ultimate gift of eternal life is something we must wait for. That is a lie, guys! It's not Biblical, and it leaves you in a place of waiting, when God wants you to wrap your hands around promise right *now!*

So how do we do that? How is it possible for us to place our hands on eternal life while still having our feet planted on Earth?

[I am writing about] what existed *from the beginning*, what we have *heard*, what we have *seen* with our eyes, what we have *looked at* and *touched* with our hands, concerning the *Word of Life* [the One who existed even before the beginning of the world, Christ]—*and the Life* [an aspect of his being] was manifested, and we have seen [it as eyewitnesses] and testify and declare to you [the Life], *the eternal Life who was [already existing] with the Father* and was [actually] made visible to us [his followers]—what we have *seen and heard we also proclaim to you*, so that *you too may have fellowship [as partners] with us*. And indeed our fellowship [which is a distinguishing mark of born-again believers] is with the Father, and with his Son Jesus Christ. (1 John 1:1-3, AMP, emphasis added)

To break this down, John is saying that all the things they'd seen and touched (concerning all Christ did while he was on Earth) were nothing more than ETERNAL LIFE manifested and made visible for them to see with their natural eye. In other words, all the things they saw and heard were recorded for us so we could partner our faith with the Father, right now, and see the *same things* happen in our lives. So how is it that they saw eternal life on Earth if it's meant for Heaven? Can we see eternal life manifest in our lives by laying hands on it just like they did?

Friend, the "eternal life" that John said they saw with their eyes and touched with their hands wasn't Heaven; it was the promise of the Holy Spirit who was in Christ as he did all he did on the earth.

The greatest gift of the cross is the gift of the Holy Spirit inside of us. He saved you from your sins so you could navigate through life safely, with the Holy Spirit inside you. Eternal life doesn't only lie within the promise of Heaven; it lies within the promise of *now*. You have power through the Holy Spirit to possess the promise of LIFE during your present circumstance. John 10:10 says that Christ came to give you life, and *life more abundantly*. Friends, that life he's talking about is for *now,* not later!

Stop living for tomorrow when you can start living for today!

For the law of the Spirit of life [which is] in Christ Jesus [the law of our new being] has *set you free* from the law of sin and of death. (Romans 8:2, AMP, emphasis added)

As for you, the anointing [the special gift, the preparation] which you received from Him *remains [permanently] in you*, and you have no need for anyone to teach you. But just as His anointing teaches you [giving you insight through the presence of the Holy Spirit] about all things, *and is true and is not a lie*, and just as His anointing has taught you, you must remain in Him [being rooted in Him, knit to Him].

Now, little children (believers, dear ones), remain in Him [with unwavering faith], so that when He appears [at His return], *we may have [perfect] confidence and not be ashamed* and shrink away from Him at His coming. (1 John 2:27-28, AMP, emphasis added)

Here are a few things I want to point out as we wrap up this chapter. They're the same things that kept me grounded in who I am during the darkest seasons of my life and kept me pulling myself out of the dirt so I could continue moving forward.

1. You are free from the law of sin and death—even when you mess up!
2. You know God—even when you think you don't—because he lives in you.
3. You have been promised eternal life, and nothing you do can break his promise!
4. The anointing on your life is permanent! That means that nothing can take it away.
5. You do not have to be ashamed in his presence—even through all the dirt in your life!

The moment Jesus became unfiltered on the cross is the moment that he placed promise in your hands. The moment he said, "It is finished," is the moment that destiny began for you. The moment his blood was shed for your sins was the moment that the filters were torn so you could own your tomorrow! His death gave you life, and his resurrection showed you that you have the power to defeat anything that comes your way! The moment He formed you from the dirt, he breathed his life into your destiny. He chose you before you ever chose him, and he called you before you ever had a chance to become clean. Listen to me, you carry the DNA (Destiny, Name, Authority) to do whatever it is that you *believe* you can do through Christ! No demon, personality, darkness, or thing can stop you from laying hands on the promise for your life. You are the one who holds the power to activate your faith and to possess all that God has for your life.

When I was walking through the possibility of having to face cancer, I found myself recalling the scripture King David became so famous for—Psalm 23. I would go through it all, but I just want to focus on one scripture out of the passage.

> Even though I walk through the
>
> > [sunless] valley of the shadow of death,
>
> I fear no evil, for You are with me;
>
> Your rod [to protect] and Your staff [to guide],
>
> > they comfort and console me. (Psalm 23:4, AMP)

You see, David lived underneath the Old Covenant (old promise), but we have the New Covenant (better promise). Where David had a shadow, we have a Savior! He found the ability to trust the Father with the *shadow* of his dirt, but we can trust the Father with the *substance* of our dirt. Not only do you have no need to fear, but you can also recognize that shadows are nothing more than proof that *light* is behind what's casting darkness on your life. It shows that Jesus is closer than we think, and that the substance of our faith has the opportunity to take root and grow!

Where David had a shadow, we have a savior!

I'll say it one last time. Jesus can't touch what you don't allow Him to, and you can't see destiny come alive until you start to walk through the dirt and embrace that destiny! Nothing you could ever do will unappoint you from your DESTINY, steal your NAME, or take your AUTHORITY to do all you were created for. The question is, Will you walk in your DNA by unfiltering the lies you've been holding on to so you can walk in the truth of God's Word?

You have all you need inside of you to confidently step into everything you've ever dreamed of. No one holds the power to tell your story other than yourself. Your voice has a backbone waiting to be heard, and it tells the journey of brokenness that was willing to be rebuilt.

How long will you wait for promise?

How many more chapters will you allow to pass you by in life before you finally own your destiny?

Lack of confidence will keep you captive to the cave of life, but people are waiting to watch you walk into authority and hear you ROAR! I would love to tell you more, but that's for another book …

Confession

From the time I was a child, the phrase "eternal life" was equated to Heaven, but that kept me *waiting* for promise.

Truth

You have the DNA (Destiny, Name, Authority) to see eternal life, *right now,* through the gift of the Holy Spirit.

BONUS Letter: *Phoenix*

Dear Alissa,

I am your phoenix. The part of you that has been burned but continues to rise, time and time again. I am your reminder of the height that takes flight from the lowest points of your life, and I am your proof that you are so much more than a scarred heart. You are a survivor of the worst kinds of hell, and you will survive more to come.

When you were raped, I am the voice that rose up as "victim" tried to claim your name.

When eating disorders, self- hate, divorce, and suicidal thoughts came to label your life, I defeated them.

When cancer tried to plant itself in your body, I killed it before it had a chance to kill you.

I am the one that put my foot on the neck of depression when it tried to numb your life with dirt. And I burned bright with your destiny when lies came to deny your identity.

Yes, I am your phoenix, and together we have raised two beautiful daughters to know they can breathe fire of their own. We have shown them what it looks like to not be fragile, but to be *free* in Christ. And guess what?

We will raise even more kids to know the same. I am the part of you that has become a trailblazer of legacy for your family to find their way back to purpose if they fall off course.

I will be the voice of hope to countless people around the world as I share your story, unfiltered and unashamed ... and I will not quit.

I am a beacon of life, reminding people that hell may burn hot, but they can burn brighter. I am a backbone of beauty, showing others how to build with the fragmented pieces of their life. I am a mark of promise, proving that ASHES are nothing more than an assignment on your life. I am an example of restoration, showing just how high you can rise from the dirt and take flight into destiny at any given time.

I am your phoenix.

I am here.

You cannot fail. ... Just look at all you've done already.

Your Phoenix

Conclusion

Friends,

One more secret before we go, shall I? Shh, don't tell anyone ... 'cause it's kind of embarrassing.

Confession #16: I used to want to be a rock star.

No lie—full on BarlowGirl, Superchick, or Krystal Meyers type of famous. Okay, maybe none of those names ring a bell for you, but back in my day, those were the female rock stars of the Christian music industry. I used to admire the messy hair, nose rings, and their ability to play lead on the electric guitar. Their gift to lead worship and own the uniqueness of who they were just captivated me.

I'll never forget the joy I felt when, at my Sweet Sixteen, my daddy presented me with my very own guitar to shred on. It was a purple Peavey, and I was in love with it, my friends! I was sure I'd be famous fast, and I was unapologetic when I shared these dreams with everyone I knew. In fact, almost immediately after I got it, I remember ghetto rigging a karaoke machine in order to write my first song. With Google Search to the rescue, I taught myself three chords and wrote my first "hit" in just one single day. And with a cassette tape, that machine I mentioned, and a microphone propped up "just right" so it could pick up my voice over the guitar amp, I channeled every bit of emotion that I possibly could and recorded my first song. And I'm proud to say that, to this day, I still have that tape tucked away in my wooden hope chest. What I'm ashamed to say, though, is that no one will EVER hear a copy of it until I am cold, dead, and buried six feet under. Ha! (It was horrible.)

What's my point exactly? My point is that with every emotional season of my life, I always seem to revert back to my guitar, and that's where I found myself when my ex-husband decided to leave me. One night after the kids went to bed, I began to channel every Taylor Swift vibe that I possibly could. I sat down with every intention to write a catchy, yet cutting, tune that would tell the story of how badly he hurt me.

But what happened next marked my life in more ways than one. The song I wrote became an anthem for my story and resulted in a tattoo on my arm. That tattoo reminds me of what I'm truly capable of and keeps me aware of the fact that I hold the power to either **RISE** or **RETREAT** when hell comes my way. It seared in my memory the moment I realized that ashes are nothing more than an assignment on my life, and it taught me that I'm the only person in this lifetime who can hold me back from tapping into every ounce of purpose that's in my heart.

Ashes are nothing more than assignment on my life.

Friends, I refused to be the kind of human that destroyed myself, and—for the love of coffee—I'm begging you to do the same.

The song I wrote was titled "PHOENIX," and it breathed fire on the filters of my life as I began to step into the grace and love of Christ in a new way. It taught me to not be ashamed of where I was in that moment and encouraged me to embrace destiny in the depths of hardship.

I've thought for days on how I would end this book out for you, and I couldn't think of any better way than to challenge you to find freedom in the memory of yesterday by using it as a tool to remain faithful in your now. There's nothing more powerful than recalling where you've been so you can rise to where you're headed. Sometimes it takes fire in your life to refine your future, and sometimes it takes walking through hell to see your destiny happen.

So let me encourage you with these final words. You have not been forgotten; you have been hidden so that you can learn what it means to be held by him! You have not been punished; you have been positioned to learn what it looks like to take possession of promise! You have not been destroyed; you are simply being deployed into a new season for a new assignment!

Although your feelings are relevant to your healing process, you must also understand that your feelings aren't *fact*. They are fickle. They will change as you go through the highs and lows of life. Therefore, you must not use your "feelings" as a meter to gauge where it is that you're at in your journey; your faith should always be the compass toward your promise.

Let me take you by the hand one more time as I scream from the ink on these pages. Friend, when you're walking down a dirt-filled road and reaching toward destiny, God is NOT requiring you to be showy with your journey. All he wants is for you to SHOW UP! No one else can do this for you. You have to *own your today* because your tomorrow is on the way, no matter what you choose.

I need you to reach down into the depths of your soul and find some righteous anger about your situation. I need you to get MAD AS HELL about where you are right now, and—for the love of coffee—USE IT to take control of the promise for your life! Maybe you've never lain hands on purpose before. Maybe you haven't even been able to see the slightest glimpse of hope up ahead. Maybe you feel like you've touched promise, but it got away from you faster than you could grab ahold of it.

Wherever you are, I'm here to tell you that you can have everything the Word says you can have, but you have to *move toward it.* You have to dig through the crap! You have to sort through the pieces of your life and allow God to build with the brokenness of your reality. You have to open your eyes and see the fresh start that's in front of you. Because, friend, you cannot move forward when you're living backward! You cannot set yourself free when you're shackled to filters. Stop replaying the tragedy, pain, and failures from your past. They do not define you. They're simply there to remind you that destiny is created from the dirt of your life. The question is, Will you utilize it to create promise, vision, purpose, and calling for your future?

When will you stop letting the things that happened to you create barriers around all that's meant for you? How long will you wander around in the wilderness before you finally realize that promise is right within reach? Destiny was written in your dirt long before you felt the weight of being dirty! Will you reach down and grab ahold of it with me? Will you allow yourself to feel the potential of who you can be? Will you stop allowing filtered versions of yourself to control where you're headed? Can you make the decision today to walk in the DNA of who you are by owning your DESTINY, NAME, and AUTHROITY once more?

Stand up straight, put down the filters, and refuse to be the one who destroys yourself with lies. There is more to you than what you've been through. You are a FREAKING PHOENIX rising from the ashes and flying into the assignment for your life! The flames you've been through can no longer make you fear your future; they can only unfilter the reality of how fierce you truly are. The filters that owned you can no longer mask your face with dirt; they can only mark your future with destiny. You are not meant to be lonely. You are meant to lead! You have not been chosen for abuse. You have been created for anointing! Your story doesn't end just because you fell; it begins when you take control of the hell in your life! The thing you've gone through has not been a loss. It has set you up to be launched into what you've been praying for!

Do you trust that God is bigger than the bullcrap you're walking through? Do you believe that the burns you're healing from right now can lead to the biggest blessings of your tomorrow?

Listen, friend, I am not saying anything to you that I didn't say to myself. I'm not asking you to do anything that I didn't do as well. I'm typing this letter with tear-stained cheeks as the journals of my life sit stacked up beside me, and I'm begging you *not* to quit ... because I know what happens when you don't! I'm pleading with you to *keep on going* ... because I've seen promise on the other side of pain!

Restoration only comes when you learn to rest in him and trust him with your heart. I know I haven't heard your story, but that's okay. Every situation is different, but the solution always remains the same: his name is Jesus! There is victory found within your voice, but you have to be willing to take off the badges that label you as "victim." You may still be sorting through the pieces of life, but listen, you don't have to allow life to steal your joy.

Consider it *nothing but joy*, my brothers and sisters, whenever you fall into various trials. Be assured that the *testing of your faith* [through experience] produces *endurance* [leading to spiritual maturity, and inner peace]. And let endurance have its perfect result and do *a thorough work*, so that you may be *perfect and completely developed* [*in your faith*]_lacking in nothing. (James 1:2-4, AMP, emphasis added)

You may be walking through dirt, but you *can* embrace your destiny at the same time. You may be scared to death about who it is that you are underneath the lies you've been wearing for so long, but the moment you start to unfilter the truth about yourself, you'll begin to find the gold that's hidden within the depths of the dirt you've been living in.

I believe in you, friend, but will you believe in yourself? You're writing the pages of your story with the beliefs that you carry. You will become everything that you believe (see Matthew 9:29, MSG)! It's time to get #UNFILTERED and embrace destiny by OWNING YOUR TRUTH!

No one is stopping you but yourself. This is your story. Own it by believing.

With all my love for coffee,

Alissa

Acknowledgments

I have to throw my very first thank-you to my crew! You guys are the bomb-dot-com and have given me an endless amount of encouragement, love, and support. From the front screen of my iPhone, ya'll have stuck with me from way back when my videos were labeled "Chews" instead of "#UNFILTERED." For years, you watched me share encouragement to embrace your purpose, and then you had the opportunity to watch as I embraced mine during a dark season. Thanks to Facebook Live and Instagram, you got to watch restoration unfold in my life long before it ever became pages in a book. THANK YOU from the bottom of my heart for allowing me to share my journey with you!

Endless thanks to my sister and editor, Bethany Powers. You are the true OG! We've been dreaming together since we were children, and although we didn't start that all-girl rock band together like we always said we would … Sis, WE RELEASED A FREAKING BOOK! You've watched me add chapters and revise pages right up to the deadline, and you didn't kill me. You've encouraged me to share my story despite the fear of confessing my secrets. You were a sounding board, a Marco Polo savior, and a pure saint when it came to hearing my ideas and helping me bring this project to life. Thank you for holding me down in more ways than you know, and thank you for helping to make this dream of mine come true.

Of course, I'd have no story to tell if my parents hadn't given me life way back in '89. Kevin and Veronica Powers, thank you for believing in me. Your faith, love, and trust in God has taught me how to fight the filters of life and has given me the strength to know I can overcome hell without it swallowing me with pain. You guys were a big part of nurturing my heart and speaking life over my purpose. Without y'all, I wouldn't be where I am today. I love y'all.

To my children, Kinsleigh and Aurora, you are the greatest chapters of my life and the exclamation points to my dreams. You two taught me how to throw my dirt in the air in order to watch it sparkle and painted my life with color on our darkest days. Thank you for being my inspiration behind living life #UNFILTERED. It's because of you that I've held on to every pretzel tie and strawberry kiss Jesus gave me. I pray that I continue to live my life in a way that shows you how to chase the impossible and trust God with the rest.

And to tie this off, I've saved the biggest thank-you for last. Brandon Holt is my biggest fan, my muse, and in many ways the one who saved me from myself. Long before I put words into this book, he believed in the dream I had for this movement. Bran, thank you for allowing me to retell the parts of our story that hurt and for being willing to share a life #UNFILTERED outside of these pages. You inspire me to dream bigger and live bolder. I am grateful to share a life with someone who believes as deeply as me in the power of grace and the freedom of choosing to embrace destiny. I love you.

About the Author

Alissa Holt is a worldwide traveler and speaker, debut author, songwriter, and above all, a worship leader who loves to reveal the heart of God through music. In a warm encouraging style, Alissa has a hunger to help people break destructive mindsets and walk in the fullness of their calling. Honest, uplifting, and always transparent, Alissa connects to the hearts of her audience through a spirit of empowerment and love. She calls Texas home, with two daughters who are constantly teaching her how to live her best life and a loving husband who proudly supports her *Gilmore Girls*–level coffee habit.

Join her social crew on Instagram @TheAlissaHolt and pop over to BrandonandAlissa.life to hear about ALL their projects.

Notes

Chapter 2: Dig

Google Dictionary, s.v. "position," accessed September 23, 2019, https://www.google.com/search?active&q=Dictionary#dobs=position, taken from *Oxford Dictionaries*, s.v. "position,".

Google Dictionary, s.v. "posture," accessed September 23, 2019, https://www.google.com/search?active&q=Dictionary#dobs=posture, taken from *Oxford Dictionaries*, s.v. "posture,".

Chapter 6: Pieces

Urban Dictionary, s.v. "broken," accessed October 10, 2019, https://www.urbandictionary.com/define.php?term=broken.

Sy Kraft, "Love Study: Brain Reacts to Heartbreak Same as Physical Pain." Medical News Today, March 28, 2011, https://www.medicalnewstoday.com/articles/220427.php#1.

Chapter 8: Feel

Google Dictionary, s.v. "hope," accessed October 19, 2019, https://www.google.com/search?active&q=Dictionary#dobs=hope, taken from *Oxford Dictionaries*, s.v. "hope,".

Chapter 14: You

Google Dictionary, s.v. "renew," accessed January 9, 2020, https://www.google.com/search?active&q=Dictionary#dobs=renew,

taken from *Oxford Dictionaries*, s.v. "renew,".

Google Dictionary, s.v. "restore," accessed January 9, 2020,
https://www.google.com/search?active&q=Dictionary#dobs=restore,
taken from *Oxford Dictionaries*, s.v. "restore,".

Chapter 15: DNA

Collins English Dictionary – Complete and Unabridged, 12th ed. (2014), s.v.
"unfiltered," accessed January 11, 2020,
https://www.thefreedictionary.com/unfiltered.

1. Promise has nothing to do with anyone else but has everything to do with me.

2. Promise is a posture, not a position.

3. He saw destiny in your dirt before it ever had the chance to become clean.

4. God isn't punishing you. He's positioning you.

5. You were created with the ability to build a backbone with the broken pieces, and that backbone has a voice that needs to be heard!

6. There is freedom found in building something new.

7. God did not destroy you. He has placed you in a position to be delivered out of something that he didn't build.

8. Feeling doesn't cancel out your faith. Feelings are the substance you trust the Father with.

9. Prophecy is not predictive; it is creative.

10. You are the biggest prophet in your life. Press record and push play.

11. Your seat matters! God assigned you a seat of purpose long before you arrived at your destination!

12. The fulfillment behind his word comes when you stop denying that you're flesh and blood and start allowing your spirit-man the ability to course-correct your posture when you get off track.

13. God doesn't show his grace toward you in response to your faith; your faith is a response to the grace of God and what he has already given

you.

14. Y.O.U.= YOU OVERCOME, UNFILTERED. Fear and faith cannot be in your mouth at the same time!

15. You have the DNA (Destiny, Name, Authority) to see eternal life, *right now*, through the gift of the

Holy Spirit.

Declarations!

I have...

A voice that needs to be heard

A song that shifts atmospheres

A word that no one else can release

A gift that needs to be utilized

A place to thrive

Talents that need to be cultivated

Anointing that others can draw from

A purpose that reaches far beyond myself

A destiny that's bigger than my dirt

A future that's full of hope

An influence that can bring freedom through Christ

A story that needs to be told

Peace in my heart

Control over my mind

The character of Christ

Divine ideas, connections, and resources

A choice to walk in my authority

I will...

Fail towards freedom

Embrace my dirt

Get back up

Recognize my value and worth

Put the pieces back together

Own my today

Forgive others and myself

Walk in love

Live my best life

Say yes to **ME**

Say no to anything that requires me to deny my destiny

I am...

Strong

Fealess

Bold

Courageous

Fierce

Anointed

Beautiful/handsome

Gifted

I am..

Heard

Accepted

Loved

Wanted

Whole

Healed

Healthy

Whole

More than enough

Able

Restored

Disciplined

Motivated

Consistent

Confident

Treasure, not trash

Complete

Head and not the tail

Above only and not beneath

—I refuse to lose.

—This is not a loss; it is a launch.

—My life is not over. It is just getting into order.

—I am not destroyed. I am being deployed into a militant position of ministry.

—I have what the Word says I have. I will do everything he has created me to do. I am everything God has called me to be.

Made in the USA
Coppell, TX
06 November 2020

40892061R00164